Life among the GIANTS

Books by Leontine Young

OUT OF WEDLOCK
WEDNESDAY'S CHILDREN
LIFE AMONG THE GIANTS

LEONTINE YOUNG

Life among the GIANTS

McGraw-Hill Book Company

New York • St. Louis • San Francisco • Düsseldorf • Kuala Lumpur
Mexico • Montreal • Panama • Rio de Janeiro • Sydney • Toronto

To the eternal child who lives in all of us

Contents

In the Beginning...

WHEN YOU come to think of it, this is a very strange world. Nothing about it is stranger than the fact all adults were once children. One of those legendary interplanetary visitors that seem to be forever dropping by would certainly never guess it could be so. Nature undoubtedly had some worthy purpose in mind when she decreed that all humans should begin life as infants and continue to be children for at least the next sixteen years, but the system has created no end of complications.

Once the individual human has passed the imposing boundary of what we euphemistically term maturity, he proceeds either to forget he ever had a past or to transform it with the adaptable colors of retrospection into whatever model best suits his particular desires and circumstances. In either case, children as they actually are and continue to be become more or less a mystery to the grown-up world, to be interpreted by specialists and fitted to whatever assumptions are prevalent and popular at the time. This can involve a good deal of cutting and trimming to ensure the proper fit, but grownups have usually found this preferable to anything so radical as recalling the emotional states of their own past or listening to what the young actually say.

This is not a new state of affairs, and in the "good old days" most grownups took it for granted that the new batch of children were a cut below the standard of their own youthful days. There was an aura of chronic skepticism about the prospects for the world in the hands of the coming generation. It is an aura not unknown to our own day. Since the world has somehow continued to survive and even shown some slight improvement here and there, there is of course the possibility that the young weren't all that different. But it's likely that adults from the caveman on have created their own fantasies of what children ought to be like and naturally have been convinced that's precisely how as children themselves they were. It is one of those human sleight-of-hand tricks that can be very convenient and that ends up causing endless trouble and confusion.

In the first place it makes it exceedingly difficult for grownups to listen to children. They have to be careful what they hear, and they have to keep busy telling children what they should be saying. This makes for a general sense of uneasiness which results in a watchful wariness by adults and a rapidly acquired protective coloration by the young. It also makes for a considerable degree of artificiality on both sides. The normal grownup who has no trouble communicating with another grownup finds himself asking a new member of the human race questions in a treble clef and wondering how quickly he can extricate himself from the whole situation. The new member who can babble on cheerfully for hours under more relaxed circumstances clams up and limits his part of the conversation to those noncommittal monosyllables that leave adult questions trailing into oblivion like the disappearing trail of a jet. The two parties might come from different planets. Conversation requires a give-and-take that rests on some base of equality, and in the wear and tear of growing up many grownups have lost the communication line to the world of the young and sadly to their own past.

Thereby grownups cheat themselves out of some truly fascinating interchanges of ideas. The very fact that the young view the world and their part in it with sparkling originality and sharp deviation from the customary assumptions makes them by and large surprising and often fascinating conversationalists. They are almost never boring except when they start to recount a TV show with a passion for detail that reveals their remarkable powers of concentration. Even then it is quite possible to cry "Enough," and they will leave the story with reluctance, even disappointment, but with no offended amour-propre. It is rarely feasible to be so frank with another adult. One of the delightful advantages of conversation with the young is that one may be quite candid with little fear of the social sensitivities that afflict their elders. Naturally this candor works both ways, and if grownups can't take it, the conversation is likely to be brief.

Candor, however, is not the chief obstacle to communication between adults and the young. The real trouble is that grownups so rarely can believe the young are worth taking seriously. Their knowledge, their ideas, their interests, their observations are compared with those of the grownup world and are more or less automatically disregarded or at best tolerated with patience or amusement. The adult does not customarily question his own premises and assumptions, and he is only dimly conscious most of the time that they are the base line of his judgments. Thus it does not easily occur to him that children may have valuable insights to give him. Grownups take it for granted that they have much to teach children but little to learn from them. With that idea it is difficult to think of children, especially very young children, as people. Their very lack of power and ability to care for themselves makes it easy to think of them rather as small creatures in the process of becoming people. Only with adulthood will they finally qualify which is to say when they have the same premises, ideas and interests as the grownups. Only then can they both teach and learn, expect from others a respectful hearing and sober consideration of their points of view. So long as they are children their elders tend to think of their concerns as relatively unimportant because their concerns are different from adult concerns. It takes children to recognize difference without attaching such values as superior, inferior, important, nonimportant.

Children are not oblivious to this adult attitude. They perceive with their usual accuracy that their opinions, feelings, wishes are not accorded the kind of respect to which grownups are entitled. Their resentment is not that adults disagree and deny but that adults disregard and ignore. Generations of children have lived with this casual disrespect, have protected their thoughts more or less openly, have learned finally to keep their ideas to themselves. With time they have learned in turn to despise what once seemed so important and to turn away from a past so little worthy of serious regard. They do not even notice how much enthusiasm, zest for living, spontaneity and self-honesty have vanished with the unimportant past. Childhood, that fantasy has painted as a carefree romp, has been quietly interred as the years of inferiority and no-power. The sensitivities of grownups with their endless train of futile troubles seem to echo the grievances of those forgotten years.

For all its proclaimed devotion to the state of childhood our own adult world mirrors this casual premise that children are important chiefly for what they will become. They are, as the saying goes, the citizens of tomorrow. They are also necessary for the survival of the species, for the proper fulfillment of marriage, for extensions of the adult ego. They are to be well cared for, trained, educated and in general prepared to be useful. Yet we do not give great value to those responsible for the preparation. We honor motherhood with glowing sentimentality, but we don't rate it high on the scale of creative occupations. To develop a magnificent human being stirs considerably less admiration than to paint a great picture or expand a successful industry. As for the man who chooses attention to his children over the rigors of top economic achievement, there is something wrong with him. His values are all topsy-turvy. He's on a par with the man who thinks teaching children should have a real priority of value. If he wants to teach and still be important he'd better head for a university and concentrate on research and writing—that is, get as far as possible from the young. In fact, teacher prestige goes pretty much with the age of the taught. We treasure the professor over the kindergarten teacher. We're glad to devote a day or a ceremonial to those who invest their finest gifts in the young, but for every day and the respect that counts we'll take the man who succeeds in the really serious business of making better mousetraps.

Our strange disregard of children as people appears in other ways. We rarely notice when we see them as resources to serve adult purposes. Sometimes we assume they are good for adults, and we recommend them like medicine for ailing marriages and adult character defects, such as irresponsibility. If parents have trouble with one child, the obvious solution is to have another. We are more or less oblivious to what the results may be for the child or for the adult if the therapy fails, and the question of whether a child can be therapy in the first place tends to get lost in the fantasy of the happy family that is somehow going to emerge from all this. In former days we were more concerned with the economic advantages of children than their therapeutic capacities, which was quite probably more realistic. The specific purpose changes, but the principle remains the same. Children are valuable in serving adult needs, and to some degree become a means to ends other than their own. This can seem shocking to our age, where once it would have been commonplace, perhaps because our purposes become more subtle.

These days we even come to think of children as quasi-academic subjects. There is no doubt that they seem less shockingly real that way. With the resources of technical know-how and the plethora of organized groups they can be sufficiently divided up so that no one knows them very well. Life is too busy and hectic to permit readily the relaxation and concentration required to learn directly from them and to know them rather than learn about them. With the most personal of people we introduce increasing impersonality. For the most intense of people we provide the dilution of extensiveness. For the most direct of people we encourage the comforting detachment of indirectness. That might have something to do with our growing concern over adult detachment and rootlessness. Our society does not exactly encourage the emotional investment of close personal relationships. They are too time-consuming. And no people are so ruthlessly time-consuming as the very young.

That has always been one of the troubles. The young demand so much and are so oblivious of all the other demands upon their elders. They always want to come first, and the world keeps finding them expendable. Yet their insistence that people, not possessions, are the source of happiness might give adults pause. The grown-up world complains of alienation, of loneliness, of restlessness. Only closeness to the few people that matter in a lifetime provides roots, and to grow roots means also to be roots for them. Children take all kinds of changes without much fuss or bother when those few who are necessary to them are secure and unchanging. They know what too often their elders have forgotten—only people are irreplaceable.

Children are primitive people. They are concerned with specifics, not generalities. They trust actions rather than words, value feelings more than things. They believe in magic and are hardheaded realists. They have a standard of values firmly rooted in their own needs and a great indifference to moral abstractions. They have powerful and elemental emotions with little power of control and little concern for future consequences. They demand much and have small regard for the needs of others. They give as they feel like giving, and not as anyone else needs or wants. They are charming and infuriating, ruthless and forgiving, honest and conniving, gentle and brutal, terrible and wonderful. They can see the world only from their own perspective, and they are touchingly vulnerable to perspectives they have no means of understanding. They are uniquely themselves and deeply susceptible not to what their elders would make of them but to what their elders are.

That is the heart of the matter. They bring their own potentialities into the world with them but they live in a climate created by others. It has been fashionable in recent years to blame parents for the woes of the younger generation. That has made conscientious parents anxious, angry parents defensive, and indifferent parents indifferent. In fact we do the same thing to parents that we do to children. We insist that they are some kind of categorical abstraction because they produced a child. They were people before that, and they're still people in all other areas of their lives. But when it comes to the state of parenthood they are abruptly heir to a whole collection of virtues and feelings that are assigned to them with a fine arbitrary disregard for individuality.

Without any fuss or nonsense they are supposed to become responsible, understanding, patient and at all times reasonable. They should cheerfully put aside their own needs and concentrate on preparing the young for a world that is not distinguished by its rationality. They aren't supposed to require any preparation or help. That is obviously necessary for serious work like business administration or dietetics, but for parenthood all that is required is magic. It's a kind of bonus dropped by a special angel into the delivery room. When the magic works, we're glad to bestow an approving pat on parental heads. When it doesn't turn out to be efficacious, we're likely to be very irritated. That makes a great deal of trouble for all kinds of other people, and the parents should, we insist, have latched onto that magic long ago and turned out a better product.

Just how far our magical thinking goes is quite clear in the nature of our judgments. Everyone concedes that in the workaday world the average human is good at some things, mediocre at others and downright poor at still others. Even the very successful are not expected to be good at everything.

Not so parents! Here there are only two kinds, good and bad. Good parents turn out kids that behave as we want them to behave, and bad parents don't. It's all very simple. A few exhortations, a little judicious advice and a handy boost from the school system—and the job is done. An occasional mother murmurs plaintively that it isn't quite that easy, but as we quickly point out, what she needs are a few community activities to broaden her viewpoint. For magic, this has those shaky walls at Jericho beaten a mile.

Parents of course—since they are people after all—often believe in this magic too. That leaves Mr. and Mrs. John Smith to explain to themselves just why everything hasn't turned out to be precisely the way it was supposed to be. The explanations are apt to be on the feeble side, because magic isn't one of the things you can explain. Mr. and Mrs. Smith usually settle for pretending everything is wonderful and tucking their doubts between the pages of the latest how-to-do-it manual. They are also apt to be involved in that curious debate of our time, namely, are you pro-parent and anti-child, or vice versa? Not the least of the dubious repercussions of this incursion into the realm of magic is the idea that parents and children are two battle lines, each eyeing the uncommitted soul in the middle with a mixture of hope and hostility. The whole thing would be patently ridiculous if people weren't forever insisting that it is real.

It could be considerably more sensible to admit openly that the interests of parents and the interests of children are not always synonymous—at least in our complicated world. There isn't any perfect solution and probably won't be for some time to come, but there are compromises that can be evolved without drastic damage to anyone. Since the young accept compromises—at least under duress—but don't often make them, this is probably another of those tasks that will have to be accomplished by the parents. The opportunity to be frank about the whole matter should however add ten years to parental lives.

In addition there are a few basic facts that might radiate some small glow into the harassed complexities of modern parental life. In the first place parents were once children themselves—although children have always been dubious about this—and like every human being they carry the residue of the past, including all their unsolved problems, into the emotional climate of the present. This is sometimes unfortunate but like the weather there it is. Since for better or worse human nature is contagious, the children are pretty apt to catch it. That can be fine or awful and at one time or another is likely to be both. When it's fine, any parent beams. There's no better confirmation of inherent virtue. When it's bad, any parent finds it rough. Who wants to look at a certified copy of his own faults?

To some degree every parent looks at himself when he gazes soberly at his offspring. If he's completely satisfied, he's probably either a saint or a villain. The average poor human is a smattering of both with a large area of neither, and that leaves him susceptible to what is known as conflicting emotions when he observes the inheritors of tomorrow. That's where teachers, grandparents, aunts and other assorted carers of children have an easier time of it. They may have tender nerves rasped by a kid who shows plenty of their own problems but they can always comfort themselves with the thought that they weren't the typhoid Marys.

There's no use pretending there are any easy, magical answers to this one. It is simply a part of the human state—at least at this stage of the game—and perfecting the human character is going to be much more difficult than landing on the moon. That doesn't mean it shouldn't be tried, but the problem is going to be considerably more extensive than even the confines of parenthood. Certainly the easy, self-righteous response of lecturing and scolding parents for not being different from everyone else has not proven precisely adequate.

We might begin by conceding that parents rarely live in a social vacuum and that our modern scale of values and priorities could have quite an effect on this matter of bringing up children. In our impatience we act sometimes as if it were something that ought to be sandwiched into odd moments between more important tasks. We might go on to admit that there has probably never been a time when the responsibility of parenthood has been so difficult and so important, so confusing and so lonely. We might even observe that more than gadgets, formulas or marvels of modern science are likely to be required to fulfill it. It takes people to create people, and that is true for more than biology.

There are two worlds, the world of children and the world of grownups. In the days of the "noble savage" they may not have been too different although data on that point is inclined to be sketchy. Nowadays we expect that in twenty or so short years a primitive little human being with all the virtues and terrors of the primitive shall have become civilized enough to bring other small primitives into the world and guide them into the magnificent adventure of civilization. We take this so for granted that we don't even see the obvious—that this is the most difficult, complex and hazardous of all man's adventures, and the most necessary. There's nothing simple, magical or taken for granted about it.

Those two worlds are actually all of a piece and there is no break between them. It is a matter of growth. The body of the grownup is different from the body of a child, but both are recognizably human bodies. One without the other is inconceivable unless the gods of the Greeks are to move into the twentieth century. The same thing is true of emotions, of character, of intellect—of all those qualities that make up civilization. We haven't learned to feed and nurture them as successfully as we have our stomachs, and so they grow in parts and pieces. All grownups, or nearly all, are a mixture of primitive and civilized, childish and mature, and we live uncomfortably in both worlds without often distinguishing one from the other.

The world of childhood is the world of our own past, and every human being has to learn to live with it before he can leave it. For everyone, that is wonderful and terrible. For parents it is only more so because whatever the headlines say, parents are people too. Perhaps we'd all grow more if we'd relax and give ourselves a chance to learn, to explore and to admit we've got a way to go in that most amazing search of all—the search for ourselves.

Feelings
Are for Real

THERE'S ONE way people will always be different from machines. They feel. Human emotions cause most of the human troubles. They also provide most of the reason for living at all. Having had plenty of experience with them, grownups learn all kinds of ways of keeping them decently subdued. In fact, there's even a school of thought these days that considers them something to be grown out of as soon as possible. According to this idea their control is much too problematic and the safest thing is to rule them out and substitute something innocuous like a new car. Things are much less dangerous, and they're better for the economy.

Children have the diametrically opposed point of view. They consider how they feel the single most important fact in their respective universes, and they have a tendency to feel strongly about almost everything that affects that universe. In fact, children don't go in much for the so-called mild emotions. They take their feelings straight without sugar or cream. They reserve the mildness for those affairs which are

13

unimportant to them in any immediate sense. It's unfortunate that these affairs are upon occasion viewed as very important by adults, and conversely that what children regard as top priority may look pretty silly to the average grownup. In both cases the situation is likely to be exacerbated by an emotional investment that strikes the other party as bordering on the ridiculous. Both parties make the same unwitting mistake. They insist on evaluating the emotion according to their judgment of its cause. If in their opinion the situation calls for strong emotion, then strong emotion is justified. If it doesn't, then the emotion can only be considered silly.

Adults are the worse offenders in this blind man's buff—one, because they're bigger and better able to make their opinions heard and two, because they've already been through a rigorous training in what they ought and ought not feel. They've known for years about those situations when "you ought to feel grateful" or "you ought to be glad you've got bread to eat without crying for cake," or "you ought to be ashamed of yourself." Judged by abstract ethical standards all those "oughts" may be entirely correct, but they overlook one rather essential consideration. What you feel is not changed by the fact that you ought not to feel it. Either you do or you don't.

In other words, emotions are spontaneous and not even the electronic computer can do anything about that. A person may not like what he feels at any given moment—it may be unpleasant, unwise and unjustified—but he feels it just the same. Since everybody experiences this, it would seem so self-evident that it is ridiculous to mention it. To children it would be. But adults manage to get themselves so tangled up with all the complexities of living that they aren't always sure what they feel or even sometimes if they do. They can confuse the genuine with the synthetic to the point that they mistake the hollow bellow produced by the TV studio audience on command from above for laughter. Any baby's chuckle can diagram the difference.

Children of course do not share this confusion. They feel what they feel. They may not feel that way long but while the emotion lasts, they have no question about its nature. What they ought to feel is a matter of complete indifference to them. This is possible only because the "oughts" of life have yet to impose any strong and enduring directions upon wants and fears and needs. They can afford to be honest about what they feel and consequently free to observe how adults actually feel. This is very hard on grownups who have sometimes spent years convincing themselves of precisely the opposite.

The young have the advantage of honesty, but they have the disadvantage of emotions that are primitive and too powerful for their fragile controls. Emotions without controls are likely to explode into action. For quite a time children translate feelings into direct action. Words are a poor second, and children don't know many of them anyway. They are pale substitutes for the vigorous satisfactions of action.

I remember one little girl of seven stalking in from the backyard with the grim determination of an avenging sword. Her small face was set in lines of stone and her eyes were fixed straight ahead. She headed for her brother's bedroom with the steady precision of a Red Coat approaching the bridge of Concord. Rather hastily I intercepted her to inquire the nature of her destination. Without missing a step she gritted through tight lips, "I'm going to pull some Indian feathers." It was a moment before I realized that an Indian bonnet was her brother's most prized possession. Like the U. S. Cavalry I arrived at the crucial moment to prevent irreparable damage. Only when her revenge was frustrated did my young friend resort to anything so ineffective as words and tears. She did not question the justice of her proposed action, and her expression indicated that she would have found it deeply satisfying.

After all, emotions are energy, and primitive emotions are particularly energetic. They lust for action, quick, decisive and drastic. Consequences don't exist, justification is synonymous with desire and reason never comes into the picture at all. Children act out all the powerful emotions which shake them to their roots. Only as they grow older can they learn slowly and painfully to substitute words. Some adults drop out of that school early and remain emotional illiterates all their days. As children their powers are limited; as adults they are a menace.

Children are never ones to let grass grow under their feet in this process of translating feeling into action. The younger they are, the faster the response. In fact, the two can be practically simultaneous in the very young. This is delightful when the emotion translated is delightful. It is something else again when the emotion is less gentle. One young lady of nine snatched a candy bar which was indisputably hers from the greedy clutches of a two-year-old who was cheerfully and spontaneously preparing to consume same. The two-year-old promptly bit her and, as if that were not retribution enough, proceeded to chase the older child to bite her again. It was an amazing sight; the two-year-old, face crimson with rage, head thrust forward like a bird about to fall on its prey, chasing a child more than twice his size. The older child was flabbergasted. How does one deal with a creature so primitive he bites and bites instantly without regard for the merits of the case, the rights of private property or the calming interpolation of words.

Grownups in an excess of zeal sometimes try to get rid of the emotion as well as the behavior. As an ultimate goal, that has everything to recommend it. As an immediate achievement it is highly impractical—like expecting a two-year-old to grow three feet over the weekend. The confusion of emotions with behavior causes no end of unnecessary trouble to both adults and children. Behavior can be commanded; emotions can't. An adult can put controls on a child's behavior— at least part of the time—but how do you put controls on what a child feels? An adult can impose controls on his own behavior—if he's grown up—but how does he order what he feels? That trite and common expression "control your emotions" makes little sense. "Control your behavior" at least pinpoints the problem.

A good deal of the gratuitous advice that bombards parents is useless because it tells them how to feel. Love your children, be understanding, don't get angry—the list is endless. The advice is fine, but it begs the question. How do you learn to feel what you ought to feel? If you already feel it, no one needs to tell you. And if you don't, the telling won't teach you to feel that way. What it can do is push people into pretense and denial which usually makes everything more complicated. Behavior is something else again. You may want to kick the boss, but there's a big difference between wanting and doing—your job among other things.

Of course, what has always bothered people considerably is the human tendency to act according to the way they feel. There is no question that it's easier to be sweet and pleasant when you feel sweet and pleasant. It's also more convincing. If it's wise to flatter the boss, the right words drip off the tongue with much more ease and zip if you're convinced that every honeyed verbal tribute is no more than his due. Since the tribulations and circumambulations of modern society seem to require more and more sweetness at the strategic moments, this can become quite a problem.

Children have considerably less capacity than adults to pretend to feelings they do not feel. That angelic innocence that can illumine the faces of the young at the moment they're planning some particularly heinous mayhem requires no effort at all. Fooling adults comes under the heading of exciting adventure and is an almost irresistible challenge to any bright young human. When a kid is angry, on the other hand, he sees no reason not to translate that emotional state into action, which means using whatever weapons are handy including his tongue and lungs. When he's scared, he's scared, and he takes any action possible that's going to rescue him. When he's happy, he shows it and when he's unhappy, he shows that, too. That's why adults can trust the feelings of children in a way that's not often so possible with grownups.

That favorite advice for charming all and sundry known as "be yourself" can be seen in action any day with any three-year-old. The only reason adults don't find it so charming at age three is the same reason the advice leaves something wanting. The charm depends on what you're like when you are "being yourself." The happy assumption that everyone under these relaxed circumstances would be kind, considerate, gay and interesting is not, unfortunately, without some rather considerable flaws. With some people, the problem is that they *are* being themselves and the result is appalling.

The emotions of the young are powerful but transient. They can hate with a passion one moment and love the same person with a passion a few moments later. Sometimes grownups have, because of this, considered children superficial. This is a patent untruth. The superficial feel superficially, but a child commits himself from head to toe to the feeling that possesses him. As with adults, some children feel far more intensely than others, but all of the young shift with relative facility from one emotion to the next as the situation demands. It it their responsiveness to the moment and the strength of the feeling they invest in that moment that so often confuses their elders.

This has its good as well as its bad side. Children don't often carry grudges. I heard two little boys arguing on the front porch one sleepy summer afternoon. What was the immediate cause of the altercation I never learned, but there was no doubt about the result. The visiting fireman announced in loud, clear tones, "I'm going home, and I'm not coming back. I'm not going to play with you any more." His host retaliated with equal clarity, "Go home. And don't come back here ever. Don't you ever step on my porch again. I don't want you even to speak to me. I'll never talk to you again." There, you would have said, is the end of a beautiful friendship. There is quite clearly no ambiguity in the decision of either party. The visitor left to the accompaniment of mutually shouted recriminations. An hour later I stepped out on that same porch to find the eternal enemies playing together placidly and cheerfully. It's a pity grownups don't share a little more of that kind of emotional transiency.

Some instead continue to emulate the young child's violence and combine it with the adult's powers. It is a dangerous combination. The inability for self-controlled behavior is troublesome but expected in a child. It is disastrous and not expected in the grownup. Few mistakes have been more tragic than the confusion of violence with strength. Violence belongs to weakness, to the impotence of frustration, to the defeat of the powers and control of maturity in the face of obstacles too great. When emotions grow with the years like physical size, they turn their power to continuity, they make their peace with reason and reality, they treasure the endurance of fulfillment more than its immediacy.

No longer is the emotionally grown-up adult compelled to respond to the exigencies of the moment with a wild rush of feeling that blots out past and future. He may choose where a child cannot. He has emotions, powerful ones, but they have grown up with him, and they belong to the present not to the past. He has grown from the primitive to the civilized.

Not many adults ever grow up that completely. Like a patchwork quilt, we are made up of pieces from every age and stage. We carry a residue from those early passions that were somehow not so transient as they had seemed. We seek from others those controls that may prop up our own creaking ones and protect us from the terrors of those feelings that overwhelmed us long ago. For this spontaneity is turned into a commercial and what is masquerades as what it is not.

The young can still afford to be honest and they have as yet no need to question the importance or the reality of what and how they feel. How they can grow from the primitive to the civilized, from emotional anarchy to the disciplined freedom of maturity without losing the joy of spontaneity and the peace of self-honesty is a problem of education that no school and no culture have ever solved.

◆ 2

Who Broke the Knob
Off the TV

THE TROUBLE with children is that they are honest, at least for
quite a while. This doesn't mean that they tell the truth when
it is clearly to their disadvantage to do so. No sensible child
regards that as anything but ridiculous. Nor does this imply
any great respect on their part for private property other than
their own. It simply means that they do not yet lie to themselves and therefore have not entered upon that important
tacit agreement which marks admission into the adult world,
to wit, that I will respect your lies if you will agree to let mine
alone. That unwritten contract is one of the clear dividing
lines between the world of childhood and the world of adulthood and the people on either side of it never quite understand each other as a consequence.

Parents, teachers and other grownups are forever telling
children, "You must always tell the truth." This is a dangerous maxim, as anyone who ever tried it has learned to his cost.
Children early learn to make their own expurgations. When a

parent asks sternly, "Who broke the knob off the TV?" any children in question respond with a blanket disclaimer of any relevant knowledge. They manage to imply that except for a fortuitous accident they would never even have known it was broken. The innocence which shines from their eyes and the unquestionable sincerity in their voices can infuriate their interrogator who has plenty of circumstantial evidence but lacks the ringing certainty of the eyewitness.

If he is foolish the adult asserts angrily, "You are lying." Unless he has some pretty convincing facts to back him up, he has already crawled out onto a precarious limb. Children habitually meet such unsubstantiated assertions with a wary silence. That leaves the next move up to the adult. If he is a decent person, he is at this point beset by doubts. Suppose the child is telling the truth. In that case the grownup is bullying a person who is not only innocent but is also without recourse against such injustices. If the child is lying, then the anger is doubly justified—but just how does one tell if he is or isn't? He looks you straight in the eye and none of the supposed signs of guilt are visible. There may even be a faint shadow of reproach at this sad illustration of adult suspicion.

If a parent says to hell with it, assumes the guilt is real and punishes the child, there are two possible outcomes. Either the kid had really had nothing to do with it and was punished unjustly—in which case he will remember it with outrage—or he did do it and was punished unjustly because the parent didn't really know that was so. The moral of the story, of course, is be sure of your facts before you begin throwing around accusations, particularly at people who aren't big enough to hit back. My grandmother had the best solution to the "who did it" problem. She went down the line of possible culprits with the routine question. Getting a blank-faced disclaimer from all members, she shrugged her shoulders philosophically and said, "I guess the man's dead who did it." Not that my grandmother believed in letting people get away with anything, but she was a practical woman who had learned long before to cut her losses.

The point is children lie to others for good and sufficient reasons, but they don't kid themselves. They know who did what, but they feel no moral imperative to inform grownups. When they volunteer inside information, their motives rarely show any relation to morality. I used to play Parchesi with my small nephew. One day I noticed that he was winning with suspicious regularity. Since this is entirely a game of chance, I began to wonder if my small opponent might not be giving Lady Luck an occasional nudge. Watching more closely I discovered that he was cheating with the smooth aplomb of an experienced cardsharp. I faced him with the evidence. He looked shocked and denied everything. He admitted his last move had involved a slight error, jumping two extra places, but he had certainly not been cheating. The game broke up with a flat disagreement between us. The next day he suggested cheerily that we play Parchesi. "No," I told him, "there's no point when you cheat." "I didn't cheat." His voice was strong with conviction. When I continued to look skeptical, he studied me thoughtfully and then relaxed into an enchanting smile. "If you'll play with me, I promise not to cheat."

The game was resumed, and he kept his word. When he had won one round fair and square, he grinned happily at me. "You know, Auntie, I was cheating the socks off you yesterday." He was not apologizing, and no guilt struggled in the cheerful pride of that small face. He was merely signaling his acceptance of the inevitable and no hard feelings.

The hard imperative of moral abstractions still lay in the future. In the meantime he could afford to be honest with himself and seize his advantages where he found them.

Young children are usually unburdened by what is known as a moral sense. They are not immoral since they have yet to learn what morals are. They proceed from the simple premise that what they want is justified by the fact they want it and the only problem is that adults so often have different ideas. This assumption is frequently upsetting to grownups.

To complicate life further, children and adults more often than not mean quite different things by the same words. I tell my nephew he "cheats," an action I state as morally wrong. He says in response, yes, he cheats, but he means that he took intelligent advantage of my carelessness to get what he wanted—winning the game. I point out that winning is valid only when he plays by the rules. He regards the rules as obstacles to be circumvented. I say winning is less important than how you win, and that leaves him completely cold. It makes no sense at all.

When he denies any cheating, I tell him that is a lie, another fractured moral commandment. He looks at me thoughtfully on that one and finally answers gravely, "No, Auntie, that is not a lie. It is the wrong truth." That stops me cold. The concept of a "wrong truth" is provocative of thought. I begin to wonder how often children are faced with the problem of picking the right truth and what beside adult disapproval guides such a choice. The nice simplicity of adult interpretation—a lie is a lie—seems of small help. Is the right truth always what the grownup concludes has happened? And does the right truth sometimes seem the wrong truth to the young?

Three-year-old Bobby tells a delightful tale of a big fire that he put out almost singlehanded and of all the people he rescued. He tells it with zest, conviction and detail. Some adults have said flatly he is lying. Others have protested more gently that, of course, Bobby realizes that it isn't true. Bobby disagrees with both. For him it is the truth and a very nice one at that. Here Bobby is clearly right, or imagination must be another item on the proscribed list. Novels and plays are not lies just because they're not literally true. To be sure, they do not pretend to be factual reporting, but they must be believed to be read.

Truth like all moral values must be taught, but neither the values nor their teaching is so simple. The parent tells Bobby to tell the truth but gets mad when Bobby tells it at the wrong time. A little boy of my acquaintance was towed by his mother on a visit to a neighbor. The neighbor had an unfortunate tendency to gush over children whom she really didn't care much about. When the visit ended she said brightly to my small friend, "Will you come to see me again, darling?" His answer was brief and to the point, "No." The neighbor, foolishly pursuing the subject, said in reproachful tones, "Darling, don't you like me?"

"No," answered the truthful young man.

His embarrassed mother said hastily, "Darling, you don't mean that. You like Mrs. Smith." She was met with a blank stare, and being a sensible woman she did the only sensible thing. She left. From her standpoint her young son had told the "wrong truth." From his, he had merely expressed an opinion—for which he had been asked—on a matter that was of no personal importance anyway.

Grownups are always lecturing children about being "fair." This is something any child understands very well as applied to himself. He reminds his parents frequently that they violate his standards in that respect. When the problem is reversed and the question is his fair treatment of someone else, he has considerably more difficulty. This is a difficulty not always confined to children.

Father tells John, aged six, that he must not hit children smaller than himself. It's not fair. Father is expressing a very important moral value—the strong should not pick on the weak. To John, however, the idea is likely to appear illogical. He fights to win and for that purpose the best person to pick on is someone smaller than himself. The idea of picking on anyone bigger than he is strikes him as the height of foolishness, but adults seem to find it less reprehensible than the safe way. This is the point where intelligent youngsters sometimes ask that damnable question, "Then how come, Daddy, that it's fair for you to pick on me?"

Learning the rules is a rough business for the young. It's not exactly easy even for adults. The premise that what's right for me is right for the world comes naturally. Its reversal is the struggle of civilization.

3

The Whats
Come First

CHILDREN BEGIN their respective careers untrained, unconditioned and uneducated. That is not so bad with the baby because he can't talk. Whatever he sees remains in the silent realms of the inarticulate. That's one reason it is relatively easy to be comfortable around him. Within a couple of years that comfortable state has passed. By age two the normal young citizen has developed a considerable ability to observe whatever is under his intrusive nose and an uninhibited penchant for talking about it. More than one grownup begins to feel a little battered in the face of this candid precision.

From their viewpoint, the young are not attacking anyone. They are merely commenting on what they observe, often with an admirably dispassionate detachment that would win the accolade of a scientist. This would still not be so bad if they would just be a little more inaccurate. Nobody really minds their mistakes. In fact, most people can afford to be indulgent of those. The trouble is that their mistakes are likely to be concerned with such academic matters as the correct

way to pronounce a new word or the intricate workings of a
new gadget—in other words, about things. About people,
who are their main focus of interest, they are not often
wrong. Worse, they concentrate wholeheartedly on what is
true of people, not why that may be so. The what is apt to be
considerably more dangerous than the why, at least at the
moment. It's harder to have one's pet dishonesty observed and
proclaimed than to consider its possible origins. To identify
the whys requires knowledge and experience and can often be
open to argument. Since the young are short on knowledge
and experience, their explanations are likely to be erroneous,
if ingenious. On the what that is visible to an astute and unbiased eye they zoom in with the deadly accuracy that gives
their seniors that beleaguered feeling of never knowing where
they're going to be hit. The seeming incapacity of children to
keep such observations to themselves puts them roughly in
the category of buzz bombs.

Adults learned long ago that observations should be expurgated at their source, that permanent blinders are to be
skin-grafted and never removed and that the resulting blind-
ness is to be flaunted like a suit of shining armor. Even when a
few maverick observations do manage to slip into the restricted field of vision, nice people know they are to be
sternly ordered to the back of the room where they will not
be noticed and where there will be no danger of their breaking loose.

Children exhibit the most blatant disregard for this
arduous achievement and trample over the delicacies with an
indifference that would ruin polite society if allowed to
flourish unchecked. They understand the necessity of keeping
quiet about matters that are directly related to their well-

being. The reputation of George Washington suffered for years among the younger generations because of the cherry tree story. That kind of stupidity arouses nothing but contempt in the hearts of the young. Interesting observations about other people, preferably grownups, are quite a different matter. Why parents who just finished telling Johnny always "to tell the truth" should be so exercised when he does just that is one of the everlasting puzzles of childhood.

Children notice everything that is different from what they are accustomed to because they are interested in this amazing world they've wandered into. They register differences, but until taught otherwise they don't evaluate them. They don't attach the tags superior or inferior to them. On the other hand, grownups have a great deal of trouble with difference where other people are concerned because they've learned that whatever is different must somehow be fitted into a proper rating scale and embalmed for perpetuity. After that they see the rating scale not the difference. This can apply to just about everything from left-handedness to a two-headed man. One way or another they have to tip the scale to superior or inferior. In the process of learning all this children create same embarrassing problems for grownups.

A friend of mine recalls vividly the occasion when her mother went to great pains to ensure her silence. My friend was at that interesting age of three years and being a bright child she missed remarkably little of the human drama swirling about her. Her mother explained at considerable length that a lady she never had seen was coming to tea that afternoon, and this lady had an unusually large mouth. Under no circumstances was the little girl to comment on that fact. She was not to stare at the lady, she was to avoid all personal re-

marks and indeed she was to volunteer no conversation beyond the required hello and goodbye. She would answer
questions politely and for the rest she could smile and look
pretty.

My friend was promptly fascinated. She wouldn't have
missed getting a look at that lady if she'd had to sacrifice
dessert at dinner to do it. This was obviously something
pretty special or her mother wouldn't have been devoting all
that energy to the situation. The whys of all the warnings and
prohibitions concerned her less. As every child knows, adults
have some queer ideas, and this was clearly one of them. By age
three intelligent children have already learned that it is nearly
always futile to try and understand why adults have such
ideas. My friend promised promptly to comply with all instructions to the letter, and her mother relaxed, convinced
that every contingency had been covered.

The great occasion arrived. My friend was duly admitted
to what was then known as the front parlor. Dressed in her
best she made the proper introductory remarks. She began by
looking at the visitor's shoes. This brought from the visitor
the high-keyed comment, "Isn't she sweet? What a shy little
girl she is." That made her mother nervous because she had
firsthand knowledge to the contrary. Remembering the admonition not to stare, my friend darted the first exploratory
glance at the lady's face. The first impression was disappoint-
ing. The lady certainly had a large mouth, but its size didn't
live up to the anticipatory fantasy. It didn't even touch her
ears. Without too great delay my friend succumbed to the
need of the moment and studied the visitor's mouth with concentration. It was certainly bigger than usual and while disap-
pointing in its overall effect, it was not without interest.

The visitor, while making sundry remarks about what a pretty dress and what pretty eyes the little girl had, seemed to be speaking in tones of rising volume and intensity. My friend's mother also was showing signs of strain and rather abruptly suggested that my friend could return to her own affairs or in other words, "Go and play." My friend remembers that she was ready to leave. She had seen all that she wanted to. She was also very proud of herself. She had followed orders with exemplary precision. The shared secret had remained secret. With a beaming smile she invited her mother's appreciation. She pointed to the lady's mouth, then to her own and putting a finger against her lips indicated they were sealed against all inadvertence.

This is the kind of thing, of course, that makes mothers prematurely gray. If one remonstrates later, as my friend's mother did, the only answer is an aggrieved, "I did just what you said." That is a fact. If one decides next time to issue no warnings and trust to luck, there is a good chance the small person will say cheerfully, "Look Mommy, what a big mouth the lady has." The problem could be solved easily if the lady could say just as matter-of-factly, "So what?" That is the kind of response that can well be a prelude to friendship. But that is the kind of response that presupposes adults have survived without hurt a cruel classification system. A big mouth is a big mouth, interesting for the moment but hardly of any lasting importance. The idea that a fractional valuation in size should make a grown woman feel so inferior that she must wince from any reference to it can only convince children that adults are even more peculiar than they had imagined. Adults rarely even mention what a child does consider important. Does a mouth, whether it is big or little, show the lines of smiling, the upquirk of gaiety, the relaxation of generosity or the downslash of grimness, the thinness of cruelty, the puckering of stinginess? Children lack the words to describe those intangibles, so grownups don't worry about the observations and in any case they've more often than not stopped noticing such things for themselves.

When children do bother to give any value to a difference, they use only one standard, its immediate utility for their own situation. This can lead to some interesting and original standards of value. One small boy I knew met a Negro for the first time in his short life. He was immediately fascinated by the difference in skin color, and his observations were detailed and accurate. He wanted information on certain items that he could not readily ascertain for himself, such as, was the boy the same color all over his body and did he stay the same color, or would it wash off? Once his information was complete, his reaction was spontaneous and wholeheartedly sincere. "He's lucky. His mother couldn't tell if he didn't wash before dinner. She wouldn't know when he got dirty. I wish I was like him." His conclusion was not exactly accurate, but he had yet to learn there is no escape from a mother's searching eye where the question of dirt arises.

His inexperience is unimportant, but his standard of value has the authentic ring of sanity. It is practical, clear and sensible. It requires no elaborate mythology, and the only brand of superiority it recognizes is one that calls forth a wistful envy of an unattainable advantage. There is no need for lies, pretense or hatred because my small friend neither feels superior nor inferior. He observes the difference in skin color, regards the darker shade as an advantage in the context of his experience, accepts with a sigh the inaccessibility of that advantage

for him, and that is the end of the matter. It does not occur to
him to equate the Negro boy's personality, character and
entire place in the world with that one difference. For that
kind of sophisticated shenanigans he will require adult assistance.

In precisely the same practical spirit, three children in a
pleasant, relaxed family observed a physical disability of a
baby that had come to live with them as a foster brother.
They noted and commented on the fact that one of the baby's
arms could turn backward and forward. They did not share
the pity and horror of the adults because they regarded it for
the moment as an advantage. As they pointed out, it could be
a considerable asset in playing baseball. Their attitude could
be dismissed as merely their ignorance of other activities that
might rate in importance with baseball. That dismissal would
have to ignore, however, that the attitude of the adults was
based not primarily on the physical realities of the handicap
but on the awareness that the physical difference could tag
him with the soul-destroying brand of inferiority. One could
hear the easy sentences. "Poor John, he has a crippled arm,
you know, but he's really a very nice fellow." Few adults
would be gauche enough to remark on that physical difference in his presence. They would just think of him as different, and they would never notice that difference was silently
spelled as inferior.

Difference that is deliberately created and spelled superior,
like a Paris original, creates no problem, of course, for adults.
On the contrary it is endowed with high value, as the price
tag on the Paris gown can conclusively demonstrate. It is only
the difference that cannot be changed, like one's birth herit-
age, and what is also tagged bargain basement that can cause

the trouble. Children have a high regard for the difference of superior achievement and skill in a field of interest to them. The kid who can run faster and throw a ball farther is entitled to be respected for difference—superior. That standard of value is individual, and it depends on individual achievement. About the only arbitrary standard is age, and time solves that one for every child. The six-year-old can do things impossible for the four-year-old and gets plenty of respect from the four-year-old for the difference.

Children are also great ones for observing contradictions in what grownups say and do. This is irritating to practically everyone under the most favorable circumstances, and the circumstances are rarely favorable. Mother chats peacefully with Father about that impossible neighbor who just moved in. The next morning she greets Mrs. Jones brightly, and says politely, "We hope you're going to enjoy living here." Johnny looks surprised and pipes up, "I thought you didn't want her here." The look he gets from Mother tells him he's walked smack into another of those grown-up puzzles that turn out to be quicksand for the unwary small one.

Contradictions that directly involve the young are not only noted, but remembered with the tenacity of a computer. A broken promise, a convenient lie, a vague half-truth are dissected with precision and filed in a handy place close at hand. To the hard-pressed adult they may have been the need of the moment. To the young they are perfidy. If there is one set of rules for adults and another for the young—and there is and should be—they have to be explained with precision and clarity. Otherwise the differences will be translated as contradiction, to the mutual confusion of grownups and children. It's always the nature of the rules, of course, that matters, not the fact that there are rules.

Plenty of adults say and believe that grownups should be polite to children as well as to other grownups and that children should be polite to grownups if not to other children. This is another of those things that is easier said than done. At the dinner table Mary reaches for the bread and Father tells her mildly, "Don't grab at the table. Ask for what you want." So Mary says, "Give me the bread." Father replies, "Say please." Mary says, "Please give me the bread."

A few minutes later Father says, "Pass me the bread." Mary, who knows an opportunity when she sees one, answers firmly, "Say please." Father gives her an irritated glare and barks, "Don't be impertinent." A moment or so later he turns to the dinner guest and murmurs politely, "Mrs. Brown, would you pass me the cream, please?"

By coffee time Father has forgotten the small incident and wonders why Mary is aggrieved. "What does get into children?" he mutters to himself. Mary considers that what the rule really says is adults should be polite to adults and children should be polite to adults but adults don't have to be polite to children. In the unlikely event that Mary could express all this as an abstraction, she would certainly get an indignant denial from Father, who meant nothing of the kind, at least so far as he was aware. He could even point out the danger of generalizing from one incident, but the young would never understand. Even grownups have been known to have trouble with that one.

Children are even quicker to pick up contradictions like this that operate in reverse direction. Adults say children should be polite to bigger people, including visitors. Mother settles down for an interesting gossip on the affairs of the world, and Johnny, without so much as a by-your-leave, breaks into the middle with a long account of the latest news from the backyard. Mother chides him but doesn't stop him, and the visitor is reduced to a transparent "isn't he cute?" pose. When Johnny finally leaves, the grownups sigh with relief and resume the interrupted story. The trouble is Johnny returns and returns until, patience exhausted, Mother screams at him. At this he is insulted and aggrieved, and he has a point. What the grownups really said to him was that he had *carte-blanche* to break into any adult conversation and then for no clearly definable reason suddenly reversed the ruling and bawled him out. That's the trouble with teaching children they don't have to be polite to adults—nobody can take it. Oddly enough the children aren't very comfortable with it either. The contradiction of big people, upon whom small people must depend, allowing themselves to be controlled by the small people leaves everybody up in the air and all the rules topsy-turvy. With their usual perceptiveness children are well aware that there's something wrong when an adult can't say "No" to them.

For grownups, the roughest part of the observational powers of the young is that they watch action more than words. They are superb realists as a result. They are also blandly oblivious to the fact that grownups are in some ways even more vulnerable than children. Adults have with long training learned to dress up the truth about their own weaknesses until the camouflage is successful enough to convince themselves and silence others. They are now sure they feel what they ought to feel, believe what they ought to believe; when after a lifetime of assiduous effort they can compel other adults to offer at least silent tribute to that masterpiece of chicanery, what right does a four-year-old have to strip it bare with a single casual sentence. When one thinks about it, the wonder is not that all children are taught the deft art of self-deception as early as possible, but that they are ever allowed to grow up at all.

They are so rarely protective of adult sensibilites. I did see one little girl perform an act of the most exquisite tact, but she did it for a man she was in love with. She was four, and he was in his forties. He liked children, but he was uneasy with babies. At the moment he was holding the little girl's new baby brother on his lap with no protecting shield between the infant and his impeccable trousers. His expression indicated a certain concern for those trousers, a concern he seemed reluctant to express openly. The adults deep in conversation failed to notice. The little girl slipped out of the room, returned with a rubber pad, quietly slipped it under the baby and returned to her post, a small stool at his feet, where she continued her admiring devotion. The other adults did not notice, but the man smiled with warm affection and open relief at his small friend. That kind of tact comes from the heart and is an expression of pure friendship. It cannot be bought, manipulated or compelled.

In a strange way it reminds me of a sad little incident I once observed at an airport lunch counter.. The counter was almost deserted except for a pretty young woman and her dark-eyed son of perhaps ten years. The woman was dressed in a fashion reminiscent of adolescence. Yet, the over-obvious makeup did not quite conceal the marks of time and fear and defeat. While she waited for food she was amusing herself with a small peg-board game. The boy had already begun to eat his hamburger, but his attention remained on his mother. Both he and I saw her make a wrong move with one of the tiny pegs and knew she'd spoiled that round for herself. Both

he and I saw her slip another one two spaces beyond to get
herself out of the difficulty. She was cheating on herself.

The boy remonstrated. "Mother, you can't do that. You
moved that peg two spaces." His mother turned angrily on
him. "I didn't do anything of the kind. I only moved that one
space. And if you're so smart you take the game and play it
yourself." She shoved the small board toward the boy.

He looked at her with the sorrow of disillusion already
half acknowledged in his eyes. "Don't you want a bite of my
hamburger while you wait?" he pleaded. His mother refused,
still angry, and opened a magazine. Her head was turned indignantly away from him. Slowly the boy finished his lunch
and then slid down from his seat. "I'm going to look around,"
he announced, and his voice was muted, as if someone had just
died. "Do," said his mother. She did not look up.

She thought she had just pushed away a game to protect
herself from the knowledge that her son was brighter and
more honest than she. What she did not see was that she had
also pushed away love, compassion and loyalty. Sometimes it
is hard to know who needs protection from whom.

Children can be heedless of the delicate and tough web of
grown-up self-deceptions. They do not yet have so much to
lose that they must lie to themselves. Yet they can also have
that most precious of gifts for those they love, the manners of
the heart.

4

Good to the
Last Drop

FEW PHENOMENA can leave a grownup so open-mouthed as an
encounter with literal thinking. He may not even know what
is happening to him. All of a sudden he is not communicating,
although the other human is speaking perfectly intelligible
English. He is likely to open his mouth and then close it again
without issuing a sound. He gets a distinct feeling of helplessness with a confused conviction that something is definitely
wrong. What is wrong is that he and the other person are
putting the English language to quite different purposes and
are involved in quite different premises.

According to a friend of mine, a literal-minded person is
one who always leaves the last drop in a cup of Maxwell
House coffee. The ad says good to the last drop not through
it. For the grownup this is the stuff of jokes and as such he
enjoys it. To take it seriously and even worse, to act on it, is
about the same as a blank wall—what do you do with it?
Normal adults simply don't think that way anymore.

Children, however, do think precisely that way, and the

younger they are the more completely literal they are. What
is even more nerve-wracking for harassed grownups, they
combine literalness with their rather terrible exactness of observation and the naive ruthlessness of their honesty. It is a
combination as explosive as those splitting atoms and one they
survive only because adults consider them too young to know
better. Any experience with that combination is apt to leave
the average grownup with the feeling that he has stepped into
an alien world full of unexpected dangers and that the whole
thing is perfectly ridiculous because all he's doing is talking
with three-year-old Johnny. He does a double-take that has
the feeling of a landlubber admiring the sea and abruptly
succumbing to seasickness. The literal operate on the immediate, the exact, the specific. The dimensions of knowledge
shrink to the flat precision of what is visible from one given
spot.

Young children live in a literal world which, like their
drawings, lacks perspective. In that world words mean exactly what they say and no nonsense about figurative or alter-
nate meanings. When mother describes an outrageous encounter with human intractability, she says, "When I heard
that I hit the ceiling." Johnny looks at her with considerable
interest and asks if it hurt.

That is simply not explicable in a sentence or two, and
you have a dim awareness that there are two worlds here not
to be easily bridged. A man says impatiently to his angry
wife, "All right, you don't have to take my head off," and his
son looks consideringly from one to the other. Just what he is
considering is rarely discovered because about that time one
parent or the other shouts, "You go on in the other room and
play with your new puzzle." This is probably a wise reaction

since what children actually consider can be very shocking to grownups.

A young mother of my acquaintance recently overheard her two small offspring considering aloud. She had put them to bed against their strenuous objections after she interrupted a fascinating project involving the use of her favorite perfume as a sprinkling device for the cat. The older one, aged four, said slowly, "What should we do to her?" His two-year-old sister, being less inhibited, said enthusiastically, "Let's kill her." The older one, more practical, asked, "How?"

His sister gave the matter some thought and then remarked brightly, "Let's put her in the refrigerator."

"No," responded her practical brother. "She's too big. She wouldn't go in."

"We could cut her up first," the little one suggested cheerily. That, her brother admitted, was a possible solution to the problem. By that time both of them were feeling much better and to their mother's surprise dropped peacefully asleep. When they awoke an hour later they were affectionate little children, happy to see her.

Practically every adult has said more than once about someone he was devoted to, "I could have killed him—or her." There is, I submit, a definite difference between that exasperated remark and the careful calculations of those youthful innocents. Their feelings were transient, but the plans were literal and exact. It is not only that the adult is not serious in his threat, while there is a fair presumption that the two youthful plotters were very much so for the moment. The difference is much more than a matter of exaggeration. The adult is not making a threat, serious or otherwise. He is using some dramatic words to express his indignation, but he doesn't connect them with the idea of physical violence. He would be shocked even at the suggestion. He's not interested in killing anyone. For the normal adult the words are no longer descriptive either of his feelings or his intentions. They linger from the past as escape valves for irritations so mild they require no more than phrases to spend themselves.

No small child understands this. When he says, "I'll kill you," he means it. He may lack the means to translate his words into action but he doesn't lack the wish. And when grownups address such phrases to him, he assumes they mean it. When a big person says, "You touch that lamp and I'll murder you," the little child can react with terror. That is a logical reaction if one assumes the big person means what he says because he does have the power to do just that. To be sure children learn quickly to distinguish between dramatic hyperbole and serious threat, but for a considerable time they remain distinctly uneasy with these words that say one thing and mean something so different.

Grownups, of course, are prone to regard such childish reactions with responses that range from tolerant amusement to irritable impatience. They know they didn't mean their impetuous words literally, and they assume that any child with any sense ought to realize it. Rarely do they see that the real problem is that adults and children start from different premises and their words mean quite different things to each. The grownup has words to spare. The child must be more economical.

A good number of grownups try to bridge the gap between the worlds by translating what children say and in the process changing its meaning entirely. Since what children say is so frequently shocking to respectable adults, these translations serve the comforting purpose of transforming the starkly primitive into the blandly innocuous. When a furious small citizen shouts at a big person, "I hate you," the embarrassed parent explains, "He doesn't mean that. He's just saying it." One look at the small citizen's face is enough to give the lie to the feeble translation. The occasional adult who responds with impetuous anger at such a frank statement reflects its truth with more accuracy although his reaction, under the circumstances, is on the silly side.

A little girl of two or thereabouts took to studying her older sister Joan intently. It's hard to say whether the unwinking stare was admiring or merely observant. In any case she remarked presently, "When I'm big I'll be Joan." Her mother translated, "What she means is when she's big, she'll be like Joan." Whatever she did mean, it's practically certain she did not mean that. The literal-minded are by definition exact and if she had meant anything so dull, she would have said so. Her reaction to her mother's cheery statement was a cold silence, a reaction which children learn early and have frequent occasion to resort to. What she actually had said opens up fascinating questions like how and when and why. I am sure she had some of the answers. Whether she would have consented to share them is admittedly doubtful, but that parental translation ruined any fleeting chance there was. Her remark is not so strange after all when one remembers all the people in fairy tales who were changed into someone or something else.

An invariable concomitant of literal thinking is a precise logic that proceeds with inexorable accuracy step by step from a premise that may be totally fallacious. This logic is one of the chief reasons that argument with the young is easily one of the most frustrating and exasperating experiences an adult can suffer. It also leads to totally unanswerable questions such as the one a friend of mine confronted one sunny Sunday morning.

He was placidly reading the Sunday paper and muttering about the sad state of politics when his six-year-old son arrived from Sunday School bursting to share his own concerns.

"Daddy, Mr. Jones said today that Jesus is everywhere. Is that true?"

"Of course," answered his father absently.

"Is He here in the house?"

His father nodded, his attention still on politics. "Is He here in this room now?" persisted the young questioner.

"I guess so," answered his father.

"Then how did He get in? Is He small enough to come through the keyhole or does He slip in when you open the door? And if you can't see Him, how do you know He is here?"

That barrage effectively concentrated Father's attention. He stared at his young son blankly, opened his mouth and then closed it again. Finally he settled for that perennial adult response, full retreat. "Go wash your hands and get ready for dinner." His son protested, "But you didn't answer my question."

"Ask your mother," answered Father, stooping to a trick familiar to every child.

But just how do you answer that question? Children understand an unseen presence, but equally there has to be some explanation of how that presence got to be present. For them it is never enough to say "it is here." Further, according to their way of thinking something may be unseen, but that does not mean that it is not material and tangible. They envisage the unseen more in the nature of a ghost that opens and closes doors and can become visible at the drop of a hat. Children have unseen playmates, detect the presence of invisible animals, become frightened of shadowy figures, but they can describe in terms more or less detailed all these invisible visitors. Furthermore, these visitors are not everywhere. One of them may follow a child about pretty persistently but if he's with the child, he's not somewhere else. Either he's there or he isn't.

My own childhood was plagued by a pronouncement I heard in Sunday School, to wit—that the one unforgivable sin was an offense against the Holy Ghost. I had no wish to commit any unforgivable sin—other sins of a forgivable nature were naturally another matter—but the really upsetting part was that I had no idea where to look for this ghost, what he looked like and worst of all what offended him. It is a source of no small anxiety to know that you might inadvertently commit, against someone or something that you can't even see, a crime so heinous that it would never be forgiven. Even worse, you might never even know you had committed it until that fateful final hour of its exposure. Since it was unforgivable anyway, that should logically be irrelevant, but I always had a vain hope that perhaps if I could find out in time, I might do something to reverse the irreversible.

In my case the whole question was complicated by a further confusion. As a small child I was considerably puzzled by the adult devotion to a beautiful hymn, the words of which were "Holy, holy, holy." Since the only kind of holy I was familiar with referred to the sad state of my stockings when I came in from play I was never able to understand why grownups were so enthusiastic. It seemed odd enough for a whole group of them to be singing about stockings in the first place without introducing such devotion to ones that were already in a poor state of repair.

When I had to envisage a truly formidable ghost that was in addition holy, the whole matter fell into a state of total confusion. Not even the rather considerable imaginative powers of a child can cope with anything like that. Ignorance played its role, but confusion was compounded by the precision of literal thinking and its inexorable logic. The moral, if any, would seem to be that spiritual concepts cannot be explained in literal terms.

The unseen is not the same as the abstract to a child. The question is, rather, unseen by whom? The adult does not see the invisible playmate or the voracious, night-wandering bear, but the child does. Good or bad, friend or foe, that creature is there, concrete, literal and exact. There's no more use in insisting he's not real than there would have been once in telling grownups there were no dragons—or for that matter, flying saucers. The logic of literal thinking simply doesn't allow for abstractions.

Adult thought would be hopelessly crippled without the ability to abstract meaning that can encompass the distillations of experience, of aspirations and goals. Children on the other hand are as a group far more accurate in their observations of specifics than adults. They see and hear everything as more than one parent has learned to his cost. Unhampered by preconceived assumptions or by the blinders of what they dare not see, children note what happens with an eye for detail that a camera could envy. They make some devastating blunders when they try to explain why some things do happen, but answering that insistent human question that plagues children as well as adults often requires both knowledge and experience. Those qualities are still in short supply with the young.

Ask any normally intelligent child to describe a TV program he has just witnessed and you'll shortly regret you ever opened your mouth. He'll tell you with a memory for detail and precision that leaves you shouting, "Enough." Ask him for the moral of the story—in the unlikely event it has any—and you will probably get a blank stare. Once in a while a youngster takes the big jump to the abstract. I heard a five-year-old, after she had been insistently instructed in table manners, remark thoughtfully, "Manners make you responsible." That is an unusual remark even for a grownup if the truth be faced. Mostly the excellent observations of the young are confined to what they can see, hear, touch, smell or taste.

They do share with adults that human penchant for symbolism, but again the symbols are literal and exact. The adult says the stars and stripes symbolize patriotism, my country as a whole and all that it stands for. He talks about abstractions that are realities. The child likes his symbols close to home— like the little girl who happily surveyed her whole family gathered peacefully in the kitchen and remarked with deep satisfaction, "It's so nice, everybody is sitting in the stomach of the house." The "stomach of the house" could be nothing but the kitchen. The feeling of unity and safety was real and true, and it was accurately and specifically located.

Of course, adults locate their feelings, too. They talk about "broken hearts" and "a pain in the neck," and "blue blood." They say, "John is so big-hearted" and "Mary has no stomach for that job." Ask them what they mean, though, and they won't respond with a physiological description. They'll talk about abstractions like generosity, grief, courage. Talk to a child about that "stiff-necked" neighbor down the street, and he wants to know why the neighbor's neck is stiff. For grownups, symbols have become figurative, metaphorical, encompassing.

There is wisdom and truth in children's way of thinking. It has the virtues of intensity and its narrowness too. It sacrifices the perspective of breadth to the specificity of the concrete. Once I heard two little boys studying the fascinating model of our solar system at New York's Hayden Planetarium. The older boy who might have been twelve was explaining its wonders to his younger brother who was perhaps six. With enthusiasm and knowledgeability he was explaining its intricate workings. The younger boy listened with growing impatience and finally he could contain himself no longer. "Yes, yes that's fine. But what I want to know. Where is New York?" That is what is known as getting down to brass tacks —although it would be just like children to want to know why the tacks were brass and what you wanted to use tacks for anyway.

When the specifics and precise logic of children are combined with the perspective and breadth of abstraction of maturity, the result is first-rate thinking.

5

From Inside Out

IT IS a dull adult indeed who never daydreams, never imagines a life where wishes come true, even if the wishes are so trite as what a million dollars would buy. But any sane adult knows that daydreams are one thing and real life another, that Aladdin and his lamp are not often seen around any more. Little children on the contrary normally confuse the life they imagine and the life that goes on around them.

With people so exact and literal this seems a gratuitous contradiction, a confusion piled on confusion. If the young see so precisely what is there, must they insist upon seeing what obviously is not there? They must, because for them it is there. What's more it's there in those same exact, literal specifications. That creature who creeps through the window when the light is dim and the protective presence of grownups is withdrawn is no vague, blurred creation. It is as clear as a Hollywood monster and twice as real. There's no use saying it's a creature of a young imagination. The young one sees it, and what he sees is there. In a way, of course, he's right because he has as yet no means of distinguishing what he sees outside of himself from what lives inside of him. The demarcation line between himself and all that lies outside is not yet drawn.

The life children live within themselves often seems more real than many of the events happening outside, and certainly it is no more strange and improbable to them than plenty of things adults seem to take for granted. A picture in your mind or a picture on a box, both move and talk and tell a tale. The machinery is different but that is no concern to a young man or woman of three years. In a world so often indifferent to the wishes of the very young, so often frustrating to their first groping efforts, so often filled with strange requirements that seem quite unnecessary and are definitely exasperating, the small people have need of dreams which spin a life untroubled by such difficulties.

John becomes a hero, admired and praised by all who know him, particularly by his parents and brothers and sisters. He rescues people from burning buildings, he kills the villains with one blow. He has supernatural powers and zooms down from the highest building with the greatest of ease, slips through sober adult conversations with a cloak of invisibility, flies gaily around the dull classroom on unerring wings and in spring floats gently out the first open window. Sometimes he's one person and sometimes he's Peter Rabbit and sometimes he's Oscar the squirrel. Since he knows who he is at any given moment, he assumes that fact should be evident to everyone else. Unfortunately adults are not so perceptive, and they often don't notice that he has stopped being John and became a dog or a squirrel or a hero.

In fact, adults often don't perceive that the fantasies of children are lived. They are experiences not fictional stories. Like good actors, children become the characters they represent so long as they play the part. That is why sometimes you can say, "Hello, Johnny," and get no answer. Obtuse adults assume John is being rude. They never understand that at that time he was Ben, the dog, not Johnny, the boy. Who answers when someone speaks to him by the wrong name? True, it is not easy to know that at that moment he was Ben because he looks just like John. However, a modicum of observation and a little thoughtful exploration can establish the fact without much delay. Sometimes even a simple question such as "who are you?" will suffice.

I once knew a little girl who frequently became Susie, a most enchanting squirrel. On one occasion when I was preparing to leave her house I missed my glasses. Since I see little without them, this precipitated a flurry of search. There was no sign of them. I asked my small friend if she had seen them and she assured me she had not. More, she joined in the search but with no more success than the rest of us. Suddenly I remembered that a little earlier she had been Susie, the squirrel. This time I asked her, "Did Susie see my glasses anywhere?"

"Oh, yes," she answered, as if that were the most natural thing in the world.

"Would Susie know where they are now?" I inquired cautiously.

My little friend nodded matter-of-factly but made no move to do anything about the situation. This is the point where adult patience is prone to wear thin and to blow the whole business by yelling, "Go get them." It is always a mistake because the young promptly retreat into a remote and impenetrable silence, leaving you to continue the weary hunt alone. Having experienced this before, I asked instead, "Would you be able to show me where Susie put my glasses?"

My young friend hesitated a second, then nodded amiably

and pulling up the slipcover on a big chair showed me my glasses neatly resting on the rug under the chair. They were right where a squirrel would hide them. Since my friend was now a little girl and not a squirrel, she had had nothing to do with the whole situation except to solve it, which she was happy to do once the specifics were clarified. Even in their fantasies the young are literal. There is simply no use saying to this little girl that she must have known where the glasses were because she put them there. Susie did. She was willing to concede she observed the action but she obviously felt no need to volunteer the information.

This transiency of identity can, of course, be put to very practical uses. Who can blame a little girl for what a squirrel does? As children get older, they become more knowledgeable about such uses and an element of calculation enters the picture which is not too difficult to detect. The iron conviction of the young gives way to insistence and even to protest and betrays the corruption at its heart. Little ones neither insist nor protest. They don't have to because they are convinced. Even if these metamorphoses do seem to balance out on the convenient side, the young have need of a little leeway in this bewildering world.

Sometimes when pressures are too great those fantasies may be the means of survival. One little girl who had to live for a time with relatives who were stiff and critical saved herself by creating a fantasy scapegoat. It was not Jean who wet the bed and spilled her food and broke the dish. It was that bad girl, Ann, who did everything wrong and had no redeeming virtue. As Jean often explained, "Ann is a bad girl. She's always doing things she shouldn't do, and no one likes her." The creation of Ann was a big help, but it is good she did not have to live too long. Jean went home to a mother and father not so demanding, and in a few days Ann left and has not been heard of since.

Lonely children create unseen playmates who accompany them almost everywhere. They are very agreeable, these playmates, always willing to go wherever their creator wishes, to do what he wants, to be what he chooses, to leave when he desires. Yet for all that, they are sad, as are the children who create them. For life, there must be the spark of difference, the tug of disagreement.

Not all fantasies are happy ones or even convenient. The world is a dangerous place, and for the young, full of unknown terrors. At night a shadow on the wall looms dark and menacing. It moves and shifts its shape. When Johnny listens closely, he can hear it breathe. It grows, and watching with fascinated horror he sees it is becoming a bear. Now it is a big bear, one that can gobble up a small boy in one silent gulp. He can feel the hot breath and hear the low growl that says, "In a moment I'll eat you up." With the last strength he has Johnny screams and screams. Only the blessing of light and the protecting arms of a mother or father send the terrible beast flying from sight.

There are bears and tigers and ghosts and strange creatures that have a bit of everything. They all share one thing in common. They are dangerous to small people and they would devour any unwary little one without winking an eye. It is interesting how early in life children learn to distinguish between the predatory and the innocuous. Already at two they fear bears and tigers, but they laugh at rabbits and even become them.

One little girl of two, riding in a car past a small woods,

peered anxiously out the car window at the tangled brush and the dark spaces under the trees. "Are there tigers in there?" she asked anxiously. When her mother assured her there were no tigers in this country, she released her fearful breath in a long sigh. Once I asked a man from India if his son, too, were afraid of being eaten by a tiger.

"Of course," he answered. "My four-year-old son talks about it a lot."

"What do you tell children in India?" I asked. "Here we say there are no tigers but you can't do that."

"That's easy," he told me. "I just tell my little boy that every weekend Daddy goes out and shoots them all. He's sure no mere tiger is going to elude his Daddy."

I've always admired the logic of a small girl who asked me anxiously, "Are there really ghosts?" I explained at some length that there were no ghosts, that they simply didn't exist. When I finished, she said with a sigh, "I don't like ghosts. I'm afraid of them." In effect, I might be right but then again I might be wrong. Either way she doesn't like ghosts. It's not too clear just what it is ghosts do, but whatever it is, it's not good. The children's confusion is understandable. Adults have never been sure either just what it is ghosts do.

Of course, adults are not afraid of being eaten up. They do talk about wolves and bears and bulls, but their fantasies are much more complicated. They even remark now and then, "The guy is crazy to take that job, they'll eat him for breakfast over there." Or they say gloomily, "Bill should never have married that woman. She'll swallow him whole." Then there are biting remarks and cutting insults and words that are spit out. It is good that adults are not literal anymore.

Children create some ingenious fantasies for getting rid of

people, too. They are often worried about being got rid of, but they can be pretty serious about the reverse direction also. For instance, they don't care for rivals such as new brothers and sisters. Attention and devotion and clear, repeated evidences of personal importance are hard enough to secure from adults, particularly given the voracious appetite of the very young for these desirable qualities. When they have to be shared with a squalling infant that for some inexplicable reason everyone admires, the situation can become well-nigh intolerable. At this time the bears and tigers can come in handy to gobble up the offending newcomer.

That small troublemaker can also be pushed out of a window conveniently distant from the ground, hit over the head with a blunt instrument or simply sent back to wherever it was he came from. A particularly satisfying fantasy has Mother finally seeing the light of reason, to the effect that she sees the error of importing that demanding, troublesome infant into the peaceful family bosom and returns him to the nearest collection depot. That happy dream can become so real that Johnny gets a real shock when he discovers the small brat still in the house the next morning. He's inclined at that point to blame Mother for dilly-dallying over so clear and necessary an action. Naturally that puts him in a bad temper, and he smashes his cereal on the floor with the self-righteous indignation of one who is entitled to vent some bad temper.

Mother loses her temper, yells at Johnny, slaps him, and tells her sympathetic neighbor, "I don't know what gets into that kid." Johnny regards this adult double-cross with horrified incredulity. The duplicity of parents is apparently a bottomless pit. He's quite oblivious to the small detail that Mother had never been privy to his grand design. He was so

sure she wanted to be rid of that noisy nuisance as badly as he
did. Wasn't it only last night that she said with feeling, "If
that baby cries tonight just as I get to sleep, I'm going to
scream." If that isn't evidence of intent, what is?

Johnny glares at the oblivious source of all his woes, who
at that moment is gurgling cheerfully over breakfast and spill-
ing cereal right and left. No one yells about that. In fact,
adults seem to think it an endearing activity. Doesn't the
neighbor gush brightly, "That is the cutest baby. Look how
he loves his breakfast." And Mother, the betrayer, beams
fondly just as if she'd never complained about anything. Unless Johnny is very lucky, there's someone around who turns
to him about that time with an inane smile to remark, "My,
Johnny, you must be so glad to have a lovely little brother
like that." Johnny breathes murder and retreats to more
elaborate fantasies of swift annihilation with provision for taking that neighbor along.

With the most innocent of intentions, parents have upon
occasion given quite a nudge to confusions of this sort. They
tell Johnny happily that he's going to have a new brother or
sister who will be a playmate for him. They have a rosy
fantasy of some distant summer afternoon when two healthy
children will be playing on the lawn, their happy laughter
drifting to the relaxed ears of their proud creators who sip
their pre-dinner cocktails in peace. Johnny's fantasy is likely
to be rather different. He imagines a competent aide, small
enough to be controlled and patronized but big enough to
handle the tasks assigned. Further, he does not envisage any
distant afternoon. He likes his results delivered promptly.
Then along comes a baby.

The parents are delighted and show no surprise at all.

Johnny is shocked. One glance is enough to tell him that nothing in the way of assistance or activity can be expected from this new addition. It is possible that the considering look so often to be surprised on the face of a three- or four-year-old reflects a hidden question of adult omniscience. One small boy who had happily anticipated the arrival of a "new playmate" took one look at his sister and hastily implored his mother: "Throw her out the window. I don't need her." It was quite a blow when he learned his mother intended to keep her.

Doubtless every child experiences that shock of incredulity at what can only seem adult stupidity or adult perfidy. It is one of the great disillusioning experiences of life. Fantasy and reality are for the young so inextricable that no child questions their synonymous nature until the denouement is upon him. By that time he must learn the inevitable accompaniment —it is the reality which stays and continues and must somehow be lived with. The delightful fantasy has shattered into a thousand pieces like the crashing of fragile crystal.

It is an experience not unknown even to big people. Sometimes they, too, mistake wishes for facts, build wonderful palaces that glitter in a fantasy sun and when the inevitable crash is upon them, they stare with shocked incredulity at the wreckage. They even seek the betrayer of that dream, unaware or unwilling to see, that he is their own creation. Unfortunately, the young have no monopoly upon folly.

Yet for both little and big people, reality can grow its lasting satisfactions if they can give it and themselves the time for growth. Johnny can see the day when little brother is an ally, a companion, a friend, when he is profoundly glad that old fantasy was only a passing dream. Big people learn that a ranch-style house may be less romantic but a lot more comfortable than a palace. Maturity comes to the rescue and makes peace with reality.

Perhaps adults would be more patient with the fantasies of the young if their own perceptions of that difficult boundary line between magic and reality were not so blurred. No one sees it totally clear, and most of us see it in sections. The young concentrate on different sections, but like the rest of us, they will live with the shadows of fantasy all their days.

6

The Giant-Killers

WHEN JACK climbed the beanstalk and finished off that rapacious giant, he showed the world that size isn't everything. Every child born must have the dream of demolishing his own particular giant and demonstrating to one and all that he is not to be trifled with.

This, of course, is very difficult when one also needs that giant and in addition loves and cherishes him. Jack after all didn't have to live with his giant and certainly didn't owe any obligations for loving care. The average small Jack or Jill is caught in the middle. He and she are quite aware that this is no world for wandering around alone, and they rapidly become aware that the good giant and the bad giant have a disconcerting propensity for amalgamating into one. This creates a long succession of complications.

This matter of size is one way all children are alike and one way they all differ from grownup people. It is a very important matter, as all children know. It is important to adults, too, but they get a little more symbolic about it. When they say with fervor, "He is a man you can look up to," they don't necessarily mean he's taller than anyone else. Grownups also talk about "climbing the ladder of success," "standing high in the esteem of one's fellow citizens." They've even been known to say with admiration, "He's way up there. He's really somebody." Conversely, the poor devil at the "bottom of the ladder" may be discarded as "nobody." Whatever the criterion for being "up there" he didn't make it, and the penalty is obliteration.

Children want to be big for very practical reasons. In the first place they are convinced that big people can do whatever they want. At least this is the way it looks to newcomers of two and three years. That is a state they ardently desire to attain for themselves, and the whole matter looks relatively uncomplicated except for that persistent snag, size. You could reach for that second piece of cake with impunity if you were as big as the grownups. Furthermore, careful observation indicates that grownups are usually more respectful to other grownups than to small people, and size appears to be the answer. All of this adds up to power, and power, as all children observe, is the key to a good number of desirable states.

Power is the right to go to bed when you please, eat as many helpings of cake as you like, grab whatever toys you want, command from big people whatever services appeal to you, get rid of such annoying rivals as the new baby and ensure at all times a devoted and attentive audience for whatever fleeting thoughts you might want to communicate. It is all vaguely reminiscent of an ancient Oriental potentate. Like the potentate, the young are blankly unaware of any such moral abstractions as justification and responsibility. Power means you can do as you please, and from the vantage point of two years that can seem an accurate observation of the giants in any small one's life.

The giants are apt to have quite a different viewpoint of

the situation and may be relatively oblivious to the premises of the young. They are all too conscious of the limitations of their power, the accompanying burdens of responsibility, the necessities and the choices with their inevitable chain of consequences. They have a past and a future as well as a present, and the combination is likely to be a considerable check on any impulsive, if soul-satisfying, gestures. It's not easy in the midst of all the complications to recognize that the small one is right too. The giants do have total power. The way they use it and the consequences of what they do are different matters, and children with their customary penchant for getting to the heart of a situation start with the fact of power.

This is still fine as long as everyone is agreeing and there's no occasion for any test of that power. The trouble comes up when what a small citizen wants and what his particular giant decides do not coincide. Then the dilemma becomes acute. There are only two possible answers for the young one. Give up the whole idea and go along with the giant's decision or find some way to outwit, seduce or outlast him until the situation conforms to his satisfaction. Either way can involve quite an expenditure of energy on the part of both parties.

That for the young is not important. What does bother them is the way the good giant seems to be forever turning into a bad one before their eyes. Upon occasion this seems to happen for no good reason at all.

There they are one fine day with everything smooth as silk. Mother makes their favorite pudding and beams with pride on the finest children the world has seen. Father goes off on his own mysterious business after kissing them fondly and promising to play with them before dinner. The sun is shining and it's a pleasure to be young and small and able to get about.

The world is full of fascinating mysteries and beckoning adventures. The giants are all benign and full of happy sighs about how wonderful a state childhood is.

To complete the day's perfection, Mother finds in a convenient trap that mouse that has been disturbing the household peace. Hastily she prepares to dispose of it. Jack and Jill offer their services and promise to take the small animal, which is squeaking pathetically, to a safe distance and release it. They set off with the noblest of intentions. On the way, however, they have some second thoughts. The mouse is really very small and rather cute, they think. He would make a wonderful pet, and there's the possibility that he could be trained to do tricks. There's no question that Mother would take a very dim view of such a project. On the other hand, why does she have to know anything about it. Rudolph, they'd already named the little creature, could live quietly in their room in a box safe from the world. They could easily smuggle food to him so he'd have no need to go exploring. He wouldn't do any harm to anyone.

Of course they had promised to let him go and there was the small problem of breaking a promise. On the other hand, as Jill pointed out, they had only promised to let him out of the trap at a safe distance from home. There had been no mention of leaving him there. That cleared the last obstacle. They opened the trap at a respectable distance from home, released Rudolph, catching him again as he emerged, and tucked him neatly into Jill's capacious coat pocket. They might have stayed on to play, but they had agreed to return straight home. Besides, they were elated at the idea of beginning the education of Rudolph.

Once home, everything was serene while they explained

they had followed instructions to the letter. Unfortunately, at that moment Rudolph became a little restless and made a rather desperate bid for freedom. Jill grabbed for him and let out a piercing shriek as Rudolph neatly set his teeth in her finger. Mother caught a glimpse of him and screamed too. Jack laughed with appreciative masculine superiority, and Rudolph ran for his life.

By their lights, Jack and Jill had done just what they said they would, and what's so awful about acquiring a new pet especially when it is understood that they will assume full responsibility for said pet. Their mother took a rather different view of the situation and considered that she had every cause to vent her feelings upon the small perpetrators of the situation. Furthermore, there were such additional considerations as Jill's injured finger and rabies shots, which with guests arriving for dinner was not very convenient timing. Jill never heard of rabies, regarded the shots as unjust punishment, and was disinterested in guests that didn't even know how to play games. Jack pretended that he had no knowledge of the whole affair, and Rudolph disappeared.

There is probably no solution to this kind of a problem. Giants and would-be giant-killers simply don't proceed from the same premises. They don't even agree on what is and is not important. What is clear very soon to any intelligent child is that the world of the giants is full of hidden perils and puzzles not to be understood until they are bigger.

This business of being bigger engrosses a good deal of any young one's thoughts as any adult who's been around them knows. They talk about it, and the adults talk about it. A big person is always saying, "When you're bigger you can play with the electric train, or cross the street or have another piece of cake." This would be fine except that it takes so long, much too long to be practical for the current exigencies of everyday living.

With their literal precision, children habitually try to hurdle the whole process. My small friend David climbs to the top of the living room couch, walks firmly along the back, balances himself expertly and says proudly, "Look, I'm bigger than anybody." His face beams with a fine glow of achievement and superiority, and begs the whole question of the inevitable return to earth. Grownups are likely to take a rather different view of the situation and to worry about possible falls, feet on furniture and other mundane matters of no interest whatsoever to the young. As a matter of fact, left to themselves they practically never do fall. Even in this happy euphoria their native caution is considerable. What happens to the furniture is something else again.

The instant size achievement is no real solution to the problem as every child knows. It feels fine but doesn't last. Then, too, any adult can come along, pick a small one off the heights and return him to the world of big feet and legs. Weakness is as much a part of smallness as power is of bigness. It's probably the reason that the young are always arch-conservatives.

They like what they know and monotony is their idea of a fine life. They want to eat what they always eat, and the adults can have the caviar. Suggest to Johnny that he might like to hear a new story—you've been reading the current one every day for a month—and you get a horrified refusal. He'll take the usual, thank you. You try to speed the process by skipping a line or two, and he calls you back, reciting verbatim the expurgated lines. What's worse, you have to repeat them anyway. Adults aren't precisely enamored, by and large with abrupt and drastic changes, but they do enjoy a bit of variety and a soupçon of difference. Not so the young. They are firm believers in the familiar and unchanged. When you have limited responses, there's no question that it's a help to stick with the known.

The smallness of the young—being a curable defect— would probably be no more than a passing phenomenon of mixed irritation and delight if it were not for the fact that size and importance are forever being equated. It's one of those things that almost no grownup ever totally recovers from. He's likely to have learned that lesson so well in his own childhood that he scarcely notices he teaches it in turn to the new crop of children.

Larry, an intelligent five-year-old, remarked on it with a certain resignation. He was leaving a restaurant with his family when they met by chance two of the father's business associates. Father greeted them warmly and introduced them to all the adults in the family. Larry waited for a moment until he saw there was no mistake. His lack of introduction was not a momentary delay. He was being ignored. Being a young man of considerable aplomb and initiative he stepped forward, held out his hand to the nearest stranger and announced firmly, "I am Larry Nelson and I'm glad to meet you." The adults were delighted because the little boy was "so cute."

Afterward he told his mother gravely, "Daddy shouldn't have done that. He introduced everyone but me and I'm a man too." He was dead right. He's a person and entitled to the same courtesy as any other person. His father hadn't intended to insult him, but without thinking he had equated size with importance in the world of big people.

Part of the difficulty comes from the fact that in certain

respects adults and children do have the same premises. They merely make different applications of them. Any grownup is convinced that most of the time his own concerns are entitled to high priority. They belong to the serious side of life with no nonsense and no fooling around. Equally, any child is convinced that most of the time his concerns are the genuinely important matters of life and the only reason they keep being sidetracked by grownups is that grownups are bigger and better able to enforce their own way.

Father sits down to read about the stock market, and he knows that is important. He may not own much of that desirable commodity, but he has a nice comfortable feeling of involvement in the great affairs of the world. Jack comes along to tell Father about the truly remarkable frog he discovered living by the pond. That frog had a croak that was awe-inspiring. Jack has been waiting all day to explain to another appreciative male what a remarkable and exciting discovery this was. As a subject it has all the fascination, seriousness and excitement of a scientific discovery. Only it isn't a discovery to Father who learned about frogs years ago, does not find them remarkable or fascinating and wants to relax and read about the stock market.

The premises of father and son are the same, but they crash head on into a dilemma. As for the theoretical question of whose concerns are at any given moment actually more important, that is probably impossible to say and largely irrelevant in any case since neither party would devote much unbiased attention to it. The most one might offer as a mitigation is a little more imagination on the part of giants, even perhaps a little more humility—some remarkable things have happened as a result of interest in frogs and other assorted phenomena—and on the other hand enough self-assurance to restrict small giant-killers to a certain specified time of their own. This may not be completely satisfactory to either party, but even the young have to learn this is an imperfect world.

Power is a very important matter to everyone, adults and children, and one way or another everyone is pretty much involved with it all his days. The trouble is that children may draw some erroneous conclusions from their observations and experiences and carry them substantially unchanged into the grown-up world. They may think that being bigger than anyone else means you can throw your weight around whenever you like, or even that the real purpose of bigness is to make sure everyone concedes your importance. This will cause a chain of complications for them and a lot of other people. The whole business seems needlessly involved when all the children wanted at the start was to walk on top of the couch and enjoy being bigger than anyone else and to feel important with those important ones of size and power. They might even learn in time that size can be equated with qualities other than power or that importance is something you feel inside, not a concession extracted from others for a price. Unfortunately some lessons are even harder for adults than children, and it is difficult to teach what one has yet to learn.

7

Mysterious
Disappearances

ADULTS FEAR death. Children fear annihilation. The two may
seem to come to much the same thing in the end but if so, the
fear of the child comes to overshadow and perhaps to merge
with the fear of the adult. They are, with all their similarity,
quite different things.

The world of the very young is bounded by their eyes
and ears. What they do not see does not exist. Real or imag-
inary, it lives only in the spotlight of their attention and has
no independent substance. It may reappear and re-exist, but
again when it vanishes it ceases to be. That is annihilation.

It is erasure without reason or cause. It is blackness as a
light turned off leaving no clue to the blackness, no reality to
what it contained. One dies of something; there is a cause, a
process, a result. Annihilation is the closing of a door. For the
young, that door may close on others and upon themselves.

When a little child is neither seen nor heard, he begins
shortly to be frightened. There is no way for him to know
that he is there except as he sees himself reflected in the eyes

of others. For a time he can be alone, engrossed in some special interest—usually a project that his mother regards with some disfavor—but if the solitude outlasts the interest, alarm begins to mount. The world is a big place, and one small child could be lost in a cranny and never remembered. He is not afraid of being killed. He is afraid of being erased.

Anyone can get a glimmer of the feeling by attending one of those deadly teas where hordes of people chatter in loud tones to each other and pay no attention to your arrival. They stand about in effusive small groups tightly closed against any possible intruders. It appears they are all dear acquaintances from years back, and you don't recognize one familiar face. After a few eons of this, you begin to wonder if you are invisible, if those blank looks that slide over you as if you were greased, really indicate that there is no one to be seen. From this it is only a step to the stage where you rattle the teacup to be sure that you really are there. The sensation is a pale reflection of the child's fear, but it is a reflection.

Many a small child makes himself obnoxious to avoid that erasure, to make sure everyone around knows he is there and thus to convince himself. The adult reaction may be unpleasant, but it is a reaction. Grownups are always saying about an irritating child, "All he's after is attention," with the implication that it is an unimportant and more, an unwarranted demand. It's a curious adult reaction because the need for attention is not exactly unknown to grownups, and it is not a need they take lightly when it concerns themselves. In fact, they've been known to go to rather considerable lengths to ensure they get it. To be ignored by those who are important to one when one is age forty-two can be devastating, but to be ignored by those who are important to one when one is age two can be annihilating. The grownup has resources unknown to the child.

Of course, that endless demand for attention by the young is pretty exhausting for parents. If children could just confine it to working hours—say nine to five—parents could do so much better in balancing supply and demand. That's where the old days of big houses awash with aunts, cousins, and grandmothers were a lot easier. Someone should devote more serious thought to working out "relief from demands periods" for the harassed mother. Many a young mother could be a lot more patient and thoughtful if she had some time in the day all for herself without a soul to want anything from her.

Annihilation is total but not necessarily permanent. The baby learns people appear, disappear and reappear. It worries him for quite a while but that is only natural considering how helpless he is. Even adults would be a bit uneasy if they were that dependent on someone else. The peek-a-boo game that delights the small one is after all only a demonstration that an important person can disappear and reappear with no trouble at all. He isn't really gone. This idea that people only exist when they can be seen or heard or felt is not such a strange one as it appears at first glance. It requires knowledge and experience and a rather complicated mental process to envisage people and places going on about their usual business when one is not present.

For many grownups this remains more an intellectual conceptualization than an emotional conviction. Such bits of folklore wisdom as "out of sight out of mind" are based on this observation. Even for the adult the fear of being forgotten, of being obliterated from the mind of another, can be a lonely and terrifying feeling. It is something like disconnecting the plugs from the telephone switchboard. For the small one whose continued existence depends on another person it is not so surprising that he wants to keep his eye on that person. Only the delight of reappearance can assuage the inevitable terrors of disappearance.

Naturally all this becomes confused with what the grownup means by death. Since children are literal, they observe with their customary precision that someone is gone and not to be found anywhere. In time they also note that he does not come back. Even when this has been explained to them in advance, they find it hard to believe. When a beloved pet has died and been buried with respectful ritual, many a young one opens the small grave to see if the pet is still there. Perhaps he has come back to life and is only waiting around the corner for his human playmate to join him. That would seem right and natural to the small playmate. The Easter story seems just as right and natural to him. If he understood the meaning of the word miracle, the account of the Resurrection would not seem particularly miraculous to him. One four-year-old boy told me the story with great enthusiasm. He explained how "Jesus got hooked by some bad men and got dead" and then with delight he added, "but Jesus came back in a few days and then he lived happily ever after just like the little red hen." There is something particularly delightful about that account, perhaps because coming back was no miracle to my small friend but living happily ever after came pretty close to one.

When the someone who is gone is a person dear to a child, permanent disappearance is even harder to believe. The feeling that the beloved person will be back is one familiar to grownups, too, but they no longer have the comforting certainty of an illusion. On the other side they do not have the tormenting confusion that arises from children's belief that death is voluntary. That belief is another one of those erroneous premises that have their source in the lack of knowledge and experience which is the universal state of the very young.

To them, adults, so big and strong and capable, are for all practical purposes omnipotent. They can do whatever they want just because they are grown up. Almost everyone can remember that blissful state of planning all the things one will do when he is grown up. There are no obstacles, no prohibitions, no impossibilities. Whether that dream is eating all the candy and ice cream you can hold with no parent to say no —and happily no idea of pounds that could be gained—or whether it is becoming President of the United States, it is all there for the taking when one has arrived at those magic years. It is a dream world, a never-never land at which adults, out of the nostalgia of their defeat, smile with the bitter superiority of experience. Circumstances that obstruct, complexities that circumscribe, demands that exhaust, batter at their confidence and competence. They stare with wry incomprehension at the small person demanding some new concession from their powers and saying with firm conviction, "You could do it if you wanted to"; "you could stay with me if you wanted to."

As is usual in these matters, the young are correct. You could. Only the young know nothing about the cost and conflicts of that power.

The obligations and responsibilities, the interests and diverse demands, the weaknesses and defeats that weigh so heavily in the world are unknown to children, and would be of no interest to them anyway. With that single-minded concentration that is so typical of them, children simply come back to the essential fact, "You could if you wanted to." There seems no good reason, therefore, to suppose that adults could not remain alive and available if they wanted to. From this to equating death with deliberate desertion is a short, logical step, one that children with their inimitable logic usually take. Who deliberately deserts forever a person he loves? The answer is so obvious that its reverse implication leaps to the mind. When a loved person does desert one forever, clearly he does not love in return. That is a bitter conclusion and a deeply hurting one. Grief, anger, confusion and self-doubt follow its inexorable logic. With that universal human need to ask why, the confusion may compound itself. The range of answers is not great and the fault may come home to add to the burden. The death of a loved one may become a drastic and terrible punishment for an unknown crime. Even its suspected existence may be fiercely guarded from the alien world of adults who only wonder "what has gotten into that child." Neither adult nor child understands the other because each starts from a different premise. The child's logic is impeccable but his premise is an illusion.

There probably is no clear way to explain death to the very young. Knowledge of its reality is for everyone a lifetime process, a slow assimilation of its inevitability. The grownup may come to comprehend the premise of the young, but the young cannot hope to share the knowledge of the adult nor to understand what only time can teach. Nor do the euphemisms of the grown-up world contribute to clarity.

One little girl was told that her grandfather had gone to heaven when she questioned his disappearance. She saw that the adults were upset. It was frightening to see these tall, all-powerful beings cry as if they had no more power than she. The adults saw only a child who was always underfoot, asking questions, demanding attention at the most difficult and inopportune time. Impatiently they told her "Go outdoors and play." She always refused. Nothing could induce her to go out of the house. One of the family remarked in exasperation, "Isn't that just like a child? If you wanted her to stay in, she'd be screaming to go outside. Now when you tell her to go out and play, she refuses even to stick her nose outside the door."

The little girl's aunt noticed something more. The child stood often at the window staring anxiously at the sky. She seemed to be watching something. "What are you watching?" the aunt asked curiously. "Birds," the child answered succinctly. "Why? Are you afraid of the birds?" "Can birds take you to heaven?" inquired the little girl. "Impossible," her aunt told her. "No birds are big enough to take you away." Then she added gently, "The birds didn't take Grandfather to heaven." The child studied her aunt's face intently and then apparently satisfied asked, "Can my feet leave the ground?" "You mean can you suddenly go up in the sky like a balloon?" The little girl nodded. "Impossible," said her aunt. "Let me show you. Climb on this stool and jump off. Nothing can happen because I'm here to hold you. You'll see; your feet always come back to the ground." The child hesitated, looked reflectively at the solid ceiling and then made up her mind. Cautiously she jumped off the small stool and then with increasing confidence jumped again and again. The results of the experiment delighted her, and relief lightened her whole small person. A few moments later she went outside to play, as unconcerned as any little girl.

There's always some prosaic adult to wonder why a child didn't remember that she'd played outside many times with no interference from birds; that she'd been jumping off various items of furniture for months with no thought of drifting away. No child can explain that danger may come suddenly on unseen wings, that stolid furniture may turn into menacing demons without warning or sign. Grandfather had not gone to heaven when she played with so carefree a heart. No child can point out that adults have been known to fear those evil spirits that hover invisibly in the innocent air. They've even been known to avoid black cats and walk carefully around ladders.

Children can only look and listen and wonder and fear. People appear and disappear, and sometimes they don't come back. If that can happen to big people, no little girl can be sure she is safe.

8

Time Is
a Relativity

WHEN A child asks you how much is a half hour, what do you say? That happened to me not long ago, and I sputtered, started, stopped and finally faced the granite of a practically unanswerable question. There's no use saying look at the clock because my friend can't read the clock or as we interestingly call it, "tell time." He's not interested in telling time anyway. What he wants are more exact specifications about that interminable period of blankness that an adult has just announced is a necessary prelude to starting for the ice cream store. He already knows better than to question the necessity of that delay. He's met it too often and has yet to hear an answer that is reasonable on his terms. What he does ask is some sensible measure of how long he has to endure it.

Since the only possible answer seems to involve a complicated, if not torturous, philosophical ramble, you settle for the perennial evasion. "Go play with your toy truck and I'll let you know when we're ready to go." It is the kind of answer that children grow more or less resigned to and which they allocate to the idiosyncrasies of the adult world. They are not the only ones frustrated by the trickiness of time, if one is to be honest about the matter, nor is ambiguity confined to the inability to read the relentless face of a clock.

To the baby, time is largely a digestive matter, the intervals of relative peace between yells of hunger. It is the individual rhythm of his own body. He bitterly resents any tampering with his own time clock as anyone knows who has ever delayed his meal when he was hungry or tried to wake him for one when he preferred to sleep. There was one generation of parents who permitted themselves to be sold on the idea that a clock was a better judge of a baby's hunger than his own stomach. Right from the start he was going to be "conditioned" to respect the superior perspective of time, meaning that of the adults. The infants, tiny as they were, refused to take that without a fight, and a good many parents found themselves shamefacedly cheating on the clock. The presumption inherent in that school of thought is the kind of thing that turns the young into cynics before they are out of diapers.

To the young child time has only one dimension, the present. By this he means the immediate present, the moment not the hour, the day or the week. When he says now, he means now, not five minutes from now. He is forever encountering grown-up inability to understand this. "When are we going to Grandma's house?"

"Later."

"When are we going to eat?"

"In a few minutes." So, "How much is later? How much is a few minutes?" The list is endless and tempers rise on both sides. The adult wishes children wouldn't be so unreasonable, and the child wishes adults would show a little sense.

What neither party notices is that two different perspectives of time have met in headlong collision. For the young, time has no objective existence. Of course, if one is to be fair, it is dubious that it has much of an independent existence for adults. To the small child, time is measured by the interval between his wish and its fulfillment. From the short life span of his perspective, five minutes between that desire and its fulfillment can be equivalent to five weeks or five months for the grownup. Patience and the ability to wait can come only with the repetition of reassuring experience. "We'll eat in a few minutes" can have meaning only after the repeated experience that one always eats before endurance has been stretched too far.

Anyone who has ever worked with children who have known deprivation must note the difference from their happier brothers and sisters in their ability to wait. What they want they grab and fight for, and delay is synonymous with refusal. Time has shrunk from minutes to seconds. Or for some, endurance was stretched until it lost its elasticity. They have stopped wanting, and there is nothing to fight for. For them time has stopped and with it the struggle for life.

Time can have only one dimension for the very young because they have no past. Without a past there is no future. Tomorrow never comes because it is always today. Only with living and memory does time assume a shape familiar to grownups and become measurable in familiar terms. To the two-year-old a year does not exist, to the five-year-old it has a vague shape but no reality, to the eight-year-old it is playing outside in the snow, picking the first flowers or roller skating in the sun, swimming and no school and going back to school. For the adult it is not very different except that the lengthening trail of the past begins to steal from the future.

With experience and memory comes not only a means of measuring time but the slow growth of ability to wait. What was once a limit of seconds stretches to hours and months. Everyone remembers that when summer vacation ended and back to school became the order of life, there were always grownups to say cheerfully, "Don't worry. It will be summer again before you know it." You didn't believe it. Summer was an infinity away and going to school an eternity. Yet you did know summer would come again because it had before and you had learned to wait out infinity and go to school in the meantime. When you were fourteen, you gazed with envy at those self-confident superior beings, the sixteen-year-olds. They had everything. There was usually some cheerful grownup around then too to remark with a certain dryness, "You'll get there fast enough and pretty quick you'll be wishing the years didn't go by so fast." You hadn't the foggiest idea what the grownup was talking about. You wanted to be sixteen, and it was easily going to be a century before you made it, if you ever did. But you could wait, much as you wished you didn't have to, and because you already had a past and a future, the present was not quite so urgent.

Time's perspective changes all through life as that cheerful grownup was just remarking. For the young it exists only in terms of what they want first from the present, then from the future because they have no knowledge of death. For the adolescent time is infinite and dreams are food. He thinks he is immortal which is one reason he can be a menace behind a wheel. Only with the growing awareness of human mortality does time become finite. Then the future begins to tumble in like the contracting walls of Poe's nightmare. A year has shrunk to a day as once "a few minutes" had expanded to an eternity.

These conflicting perspectives of time cause a great deal of confusion. Grownups who are not very imaginative in such matters persist in considering their experience of time as the only valid one and act as if any sensible child should be able to imbibe it, presumably by some mysterious process of osmosis, without unnecessary fuss. This leads to a great many unnecessary irritations for both sides and upon occasion, some serious heartache for the young. Some adult is always explaining with scarcely veiled impatience to an apprehensive child, "This won't take long," meaning, what is twenty minutes in the majestic perspective of thirty years. The child correctly regards this kind of thing with strong suspicion. He doesn't have thirty years, and in the perspective of three birthdays, twenty minutes can expand to alarming proportions.

We tell him to sit still fifteen minutes and he acts as if we had condemned him to immobility for a year. We tell him to be "good," we'll only be gone a couple of hours, and he acts as if we're about to embark on a tour of the world. We tell the adolescent he isn't old enough to drive a car, and he acts as if we'd deprived him of life, liberty and the pursuit of happiness.

What can be done about all this is something else again. It would probably help if adults spent a little more time remembering their own early past and how differently they told time in those days. They will still get irritated, but they might be less impatient. When they tell the young to pick up their toys "right now" and experience the almost inevitable frustration of delay, they might feel a spark of empathy for the equally inevitable frustrations of the small on substituting what can be right now for what must be waited for. If Johnny has to wait a half hour to start on a cherished visit, there can be interests closer at hand to drop the tension a little. It won't be a perfect answer, but it helps. The answer in the end has to rest with time but adults might spend a little more of their precious hoard softening the bumps and steering around the collisions of that inevitable process.

Perhaps nothing the grown-up world could do would help so much as respecting the fact that the differences are real. We set up rules by our perspective and are impatient, angry or patronizing when the young do not fit them. A friend of mine arrived in this country as a refugee with her husband and three-year-old daughter. They had traveled through danger, fear, deprivation, constant uncertainty. Through it all the baby had endured without losing her zest for the gift of life. They had scarcely settled here in safety when the little girl became ill with diphtheria. She had to be hospitalized at once. Her mother asked timorously if she could stay in the hospital and care for her daughter. That, she was told, was impossible. Then she asked if the child could take a cloth doll that was her special friend and comfort. That also was against the rules. As the hospital explained, the child would only need to be away three weeks, there was no real danger, and Mother could look at her through the protecting glass at stated intervals. What, after all, is three weeks—assuredly nothing to warrant a fracture of the rules.

Only as the mother told me long afterward, five years later the child was still recovering from the wasteland of that experience. To the little girl it had been the desertion of everything she knew and loved for a time equivalent to a life-time. Days, weeks and discharge dates were as meaningless to the child as a millennium would be to an adult condemned to sit one out in isolation. To the hospital it was three weeks in a busy routine of endless weeks and medical rules. Perhaps nothing could have been changed if adults had known and thought, but perhaps there might have been ways to mitigate the suffering of incomprehension. The residue of fear and the crack in the unthinking foundation of trust are real too.

These days the adult world is prone to treat time as a kind of jailor that clocks the activities of each hour with a relentless check list. There is small leeway for the time schedules of individual growth. What a child is supposed to be, to do, to become, is neatly tailored to fit the time slots of the average. Of course, time and our expectations of human growth are equated. The one-year-old is different from the five-year-old. The trouble comes when we try to make that equation so precise that we ride roughshod over the individual child's need of time. For him, then, time becomes a tyrant that tells him by what hour he must have learned, achieved, complied with the standard.

We're in too much of a hurry to allow time and the nature of the individual to find their own equation. In the process we often do much harm to children. The tremendous achievement of language can become a failure because Johnny's own time schedule was six months slower than that of his playmate next door. The great equation of time and growth has become an endurance contest, a competitive race. Time has come to have some strange magic divorced from the use we make of it.

It can lead to the glib distortion expressed by a sixteen-year-old girl I once knew. She had been before the Juvenile Court for truancy, running away from an unhappy home and having a sexual affair. She was precocious, intelligent and confused. She had a neat way of capsuling a half-truth into a whole plausibility that would have done credit to her elders. She remarked one day, while discussing the various vicissitudes of her life, that her real problem was her age. With considerable acuity she pointed out that none of her behavior would be considered delinquent, or at least sufficiently so to attract court attention, if she were twenty-one. Ergo her real problem was not her behavior but her age. She overlooked conveniently that somewhat more than a lapse of time was supposed to occur during the intervening five years.

Her favorite dream was that she'd go to sleep at sixteen and wake up at age twenty-one, the magical date of independence. She was going to be a condensed female Rip Van Winkle. Time for her had become an arbitrary manipulation of the adult world without regard for the realities as she saw them. Time was a vacuum divided into artificial segments without a rationale she could comprehend and without a substance she could relate to her own experience. For all her seeming sophistication and her undoubted intelligence, her perspective of time did not differ materially from that of the three-year-old. How much is five years? How much is half an hour?

Time can be friend or enemy, for children as well as grownups. It can be personal and ruthlessly impersonal. It can be master and servant. But it makes a shabby god. It is the adult who talks about using time, saving time, killing time. His very expressions betray his knowledge of human mortality. The child does not talk about time. He only notices it at adult insistence. When he's playing and enjoying himself, he deafens his ears to adult cries of, "Come home right now." One of the truly frustrating experiences universal to parenthood is yelling one's self hoarse. "Johnny, come home! Dinner!"—only to have Johnny appear ten or fifteen minutes later to explain aggrievedly, "I didn't hear you. How could I know what time it was?" Or, on the reverse side, he's brought up short when he wants to do something "now" and adults say "later." Time for the child is adult interference, the arbitrariness of big people who always seem to have everything backward.

9

Machiavelli
Lives On

THERE IS an impression floating about these days that the wiles of manipulation were invented by Madison Avenue. There is also a rather vague conviction that this state of affairs is up to no good. In effect, the confidence man has been brought to a high polish and cloaked with legality plus an uneasy prestige. The conviction has some good grounds for its foreboding, but whatever the modern polish, manipulation is not new. It is an ancient art that in its time has been put to good uses and bad. Children know it well and are among its shrewdest practitioners.

Like the members of any minority group—and power not numbers tells the story—they have to seek their advantages where they can find them. Since they can't compel adults to do what they want, they turn to the time-tested device of exploiting or trying to exploit the weaknesses of those superior beings. The real test of course is to do it with such grace and charm that grownups either only dimly suspect it is happening or are only amused when they do know it. That takes quite a bit of doing because children have few words at their command and in any case have to act things out rather than talk them out. Words can easily be used as smoke screens and can be made to perform all kinds of tricks, but actions carry their own integrity. It is one reason the manipulations of the young are more honest than the tortuous verbosities common to their elders.

Children have a number of urgent needs for the sinuous effectiveness of manipulation. In a world of complicated do's and don'ts, many of which fail to make any immediate sense to newcomers, a member of the young is forever doing someing which promises to get him into trouble with the powers that be. One young man of three who accompanied an adult guest on an errand found the gadgets on the dashboard of her car endlessly fascinating. While they were stopped at a store he decided to explore. This understandably made the guest nervous. She made her "no touch" loud and clear. The trouble was that like the substitute teacher she lacked the fine backing of continued authority. Her small companion found the temptation to investigate irresistible and with reckless abandon indulged himself. Since the situation was deteriorating rapidly, the guest called it a day and headed for home. She had scarcely brought the car to a stop before the young man burst out the door and headed on a dead run for the house.

Somewhat surprised the guest followed more slowly and appeared on the scene just in time to hear him explaining the whole situation to his mother. "I was a very bad boy," he was stating.

"Why? What did you do?" asked his mother.

Accurately he described what he had done. Then he

waited with a certain wariness for her reaction. He had not misjudged her.

She looked at him with a mixture of helplessness, amusement and what-do-I do-now questioning. "That wasn't very nice of you, was it?" she queried.

"No, it wasn't," he agreed promptly.

"Is that the way you're going to behave every time Mary is good enough to take you along?"

"No. I won't do it again. I promise." The glibness of that promise was immediately suspect to any perceptive adult. But what are you going to do? Insist he doesn't mean it when he insists he does?

His mother settled for admonition. "Don't you ever do that again."

"Never," said the three-year-old, whose idea of time did not stretch beyond the next impulse. With that he considered the subject closed and turned to new distractions.

None of this, of course, had anything to do with honesty as such. It was a matter of intelligence. By age three this bright young man had already observed that when your crime was certain to be discovered anyway, there was considerable advantage to be gained by a voluntary confession. With certain adults at least, it practically amounted to a full exoneration. He was too wise to advance any mitigating explanations even if he had had the words for them. He saw correctly that this was a case for the truth and nothing but the truth and throw yourself on the mercy of the court— with a certain accompanying complacence, it must be admitted.

All of this requires careful study and observation, of course. Adults differ considerably, and no simple general rule can be expected to be effective in every situation. The strengths and weaknesses of each vital grownup must be studied individually, and the proper approach devised accordingly. One small girl was well aware that the commands of her young mother could with reasonable safety be disregarded up to a point. Her mother would certainly yell at her, even threaten specific punishment, but would be unlikely to take more drastic action provided the particular infraction of order was not repeated beyond a certain number of times. The problem was to know in advance what that number was, and this was not so simple because that could vary with factors having nothing to do with the little girl's behavior. Successful evaluation under these circumstances requires a good bit of concentrated observation with a sharp eye for the tell-tale signs of the "this is it" point. Sooner or later even the brightest child gets careless and overshoots the mark or gets involved in paying off a few scores of his own and permits emotion to blind him to the danger signs. Whatever the cause the little girl did one day travel beyond the danger point.

Her mother announced firmly that she was reporting the whole matter to Father when he came home from work. Father represented a very different kind of problem, as the small girl knew very well. There was no question with him of exploiting endurance and indulgence and no danger point to be evaluated. When he gave an order it was wise to consider it serious from the start. There was also no doubt that he would consider her behavior questionable. She tried first coaxing her mother into a change of heart. She promised to emulate the angels from that point on for the rest of her days. Her mother refused to be budged and worse, would not even discuss it. That made it serious.

The child's fear was genuine. It is no small matter to have both your mother and father mad at you. Something had to be done, and some manipulative approach was the only solution possible. At this crucial stage the little girl also saw the advantage of voluntary confession, but she combined it with those feminine wiles nature has bestowed upon the female of the species. Meeting her father at the door she ran to him with outstretched arms while tears of anxiety overflowed.

Father picked her up in his arms and asked anxiously, "What happened to my little girl? Did you hurt yourself?"

The little girl buried her head in his shoulder and whispered between sobs, "No, but I've been a very bad girl."

Promptly Father sat down, cuddled her in his arms and said gently, "Tell me what happened. What did you do that was so bad?" Although Father was not aware of it, his voice already said, "What could a sweet innocent like this do that could be bad?" The little girl was now crying tears of relief as she recounted the sins of the day.

Her mother watched with a certain skepticism and remarked to her husband, "You're spoiling that child." He shook his head indignantly and settled for the perennial plea. "You won't do it again, will you?"

"Never," said the small girl, who had not yet reached her third birthday.

Any child knows that seducing adults is one of the best means for getting those precious privileges or diverting parental wrath. It has the great advantage of leaving all parties involved pleased with themselves. The pathos of helplessness, the wistful charm of a smile, the pathetic glint of a tear, the feel of a soft, young cheek against your own, the moist whisper of a kiss and almost any adult with a heart feels that it is no less than virtue to succumb to so charming a suppliant. Even the knowledge that the small seducer is not innocent of guile fails to provide much protection. To grant what he wants seems little enough. The small person is happy, too. Not only does he have what he wanted but along with the warmth of his affection, however genuine, he has tasted the exhilaration of power. People may be bigger than he is, but size isn't everything.

He is not phony, either, as adults sometimes are. It takes him quite a few years to learn that grown-up device of behaving one way and feeling another. It is just that necessity raises the temperature of love for the moment and puts it in the service of self-preservation. His love is a bit on the primitive side anyway and not too easily distinguishable from need. Need he has, and not too many ways of meeting it either, particularly at the moment when friend and enemy are one. There are times in life when lack of power is the only means to a little acquisition of it.

The small girl had learned more than the gentle art of seduction. She had neatly stumbled on that device, dear to the hearts of all children, known in the adult world as divide and conquer. When there are two powers, there is always the possibility they may cancel each other out. Every bright child knows that is a situation that can be exploited for all kinds of purposes. It does not take the young long to learn that what one power refuses the other may grant unhesitatingly. With enough finesse each may even be kept in relative ignorance of just how successfully the scheme is working.

I know one young lady who managed to consume an extraordinary number of ice cream cones by a little thoughtful observation and planning. If she asked her mother for a dime, her mother always wanted to know why she needed it. This kind of questioning can lead to all kinds of complications and usually ends badly. Her father, on the other hand, parted with small change with a cheerful indifference to its destination that could only endear him to any member of the very junior set. The necessary skill was to catch him alone well beyond earshot of any potential questioner and to be reasonably cautious in the final consummation of the expenditure. In this, the young lady was quite ingenious.

What is wrong with wanting to walk to the store with Daddy? She can keep him company and be out from under foot. If her luck holds, Mother won't even think to say, "Don't buy her anything to eat. You'll spoil her dinner." Even with that handicap, there is always the good chance Father will get interested in something along the way or meet someone he knows. When a small murmur asks about a dime, he hands it over absentmindedly. Usually he doesn't even notice the faint traces of chocolate that linger around a satisfied mouth.

Perhaps it was of situations like this that a four-year-old friend of mine was thinking when he came up with a surprising observation. He was cheerfully singing that old song favorite about "Don't fence me in" while he worked intently on a puzzle. He broke off in the middle of a word to remark, "You can't anyway."

"You can't what?" I asked.

"You can't fence anybody in. They always get out if they want to. Am I right?"

"Of course you're right," I muttered, and wanted to add, "But how did you know that?" He'd already returned to his peaceful off-key singing and his puzzle and obviously saw nothing remarkable about the idea. I suppose he was thinking of ice cream cones while I was pondering philosophy, but to this day I can't be sure he hadn't observed the connection between the two. The young can be very surprising.

Divide and conquer can be distinctly useful, but except in small matters it can be a two-edged sword. The young use it only unhappily when more than ice cream cones are at stake. What they gain too often turns out to be less than what they lose. To get caught in the middle between two powers can be pretty frightening when one has no power to control either. It is a weakness to be exploited with relish only when one knows that immediately beyond stands a solid front. Children have even been known to bounce against that front for the sheer satisfaction of learning again that it holds.

The resources of manipulation are as varied as human weakness. One that often ends in confusion is the stampede of the young through the door of adult indecision. Bobbie says, "Can I go next door to play with Johnny?" Mother, in the midst of baking a cake, says absently, "I'll see." When she looks again, Bobbie is gone.

Afterward she says with indignation, "Why did you go next door without telling me?"

Bobbie looks shocked and says with firm conviction, "But you told me I could go."

The argument is endless and can come to no good. The adult assumes a "maybe" is really a "maybe." The young take it for granted that any adult indecision is to be interpreted in the fashion most conducive to the gratification of their own wishes. True, they never linger to put that assumption to the test if there is any means of avoiding it. Also, it is expedient to be as inconspicuous as prompt in availing oneself of the loophole. There is no use tempting fate which may turn on you any moment.

All of this tends to make grownups a little suspicious. They have an uneasy feeling that they've been had. Yet the innocent righteousness that shines from the eyes of a child so beset by adult inconsistency leaves almost any grownup with the troubling doubt that perhaps he did say yes after all. This is one of those arguments that simply cannot be won, and the only solution is to avoid all "maybes" and "I'll sees." Even that is not foolproof with some of the more alert members of the younger set.

These are the ones probably destined for a brilliant legal career. They can spot even an inflection that bodes some hidden indecision and proceed to attack with relentless tenacity. A parent says innocently, "It's time for you to go to bed."

"Why?" says the four-year-old.

"Because it's seven o'clock," the parent answers reasonably.

"Show me where the clock says that," incites the future prosecutor. If he tells time perfectly well, he can always point out that the clock in the kitchen says five minutes to seven. When that particular problem is exhausted, he suddenly remembers that three nights ago he went to bed five minutes early and therefore is now entitled to stay up five minutes later. If the besieged parent points out that five minutes is already gone, he only learns that time spent arguing doesn't count. Even if by some miracle the parent wins that round, he discovers that victory has turned to ashes in his hand. The four-year-old merely shifts his ground and renews the attack from a different direction. When you think about it, it is a pity that so much forensic skill is wasted on such trivial projects. But that of course is strictly an adult point of view. No four-year-old regards any such project as trivial, even if all he wins after all is five minutes.

In the process he employs a number of approaches well known to manipulators. Not only does he leap at the first faint suggestion of indecision, but he proceeds to try to corner the word-users with their own weapons, counting on his impeccable logic and his remarkable facility for shifting premises to compensate for his rather meager vocabulary. It is astonishing how much time he can consume with no apparent strain before adult patience snaps. Even then he has a host of delaying tactics at his command. Every parent knows about the last trip to the bathroom, the last drink, the last bright conversational gambit.

Whether the situation is reluctance to leave adult company or any one of the myriad likes, dislikes, wants or fears of childhood, the techniques of manipulation can follow only the few possibilities. Toward those who hold the final power the young can employ seduction and distraction, can exploit disunity, can ignore the tentative and dash over the indecisive, can wear down endurance by any number of devices, can even seek to turn reason itself to their own ends. Parents have been known to wonder whether with all their advantages they're really breaking even.

So long as the young require the services of manipulation only for the ice cream cones of childhood, they do little more than sharpen their wits and try the patience of their elders. Manipulation is a part of life and can grow into what adults call tact and diplomacy, a way of rubbing some of the sharp corners from human contacts. When children must seek through manipulation the continuing and vital needs of life, they are no longer playing a game. They are caught in a desperate struggle which they have no chance of winning.

The child who employs his ingenuity to postpone the inevitability of bedtime is playing a game, however intently. The child who fears going to bed because he has no certainty of parental protection against the ghosts of the night is fighting for life. The child who tiptoes in to watch the grown-up party from which he has been banished to bed and counts on his charm to distract parental prohibition is having a lighthearted fling and nothing much lost. The child who screams with rage and fear when his parents go because he feels no surety of their return has no room for the spice of adventure.

When I was young, I loved to steal candy kept in a flowery box in an old-fashioned front parlor. It was one of those fascinating rooms with drawn shades and glass cases full of stuffed birds and small animals that no longer exist. Used only for company it was a perfect retreat for a child. To the lure of its fascinating contents was added the delightful excitement of the forbidden. No child was supposed to be in there. The box of candy was the unexpected bonus, like buried treasure in an abandoned house. With great care I scouted the environs before slipping into the quiet dimness of that room and deftly extricating two or three luscious chocolates. I carefully restricted the number in hope that the loss of so small a number might well go unobserved in case of adult investigation. Since I dropped by at least once a day, it is dubious that this theory had much to recommend it. But like all children I believed that sufficient unto the day was the danger thereof.

It was not until long afterward that it occurred to me to wonder that there was always candy in the box. Like the cup in the fairytale that was never empty it simply replenished itself, and I remained happy with my successful career in crime. This was a game, a happy game, which as I realized much later, my grandmother quietly helped me play. She understood that every child needs a little larceny.

When the manipulations of childhood are a little larceny, they may grow and change with the child into qualities useful and admired in the grown-up world. When they are the futile struggle for love and concern and protection, they may become the warped and ruthless machinations of adults who seek in the advantages of power what they could never win as children. No child can manipulate his own survival as a person, and no child should be compelled to try.

Perhaps even for adults that is the real question.

10

The Geography
of Words

LANGUAGE IS fascinating. Most of us use it a good share of our waking moments and never think of it at all. This may be just as well because language is a glass showcase of some of our more unwitting vices and virtues, and could be disconcerting if we noticed it. Children, however, are particularly capable as observers and are always on the alert for any item of information that promises to be useful.

Thus, they hear Father say, "That bill didn't get paid," or Mother remark, "Those car keys have gotten lost again." This is a tricky way of stating a fact without acknowledging any personal connection with it. The difference between "I didn't pay that bill," and "That bill didn't get paid," is immediately obvious to any discerning person and the advantage of the latter phraseology is clear. It presents the simple truth without evasion or distortion but leaves it tranquilly in mid-air without bothering anyone with awkward connections. It provides a comfortable insulation between an unfortunate situation and its perpetrator. The situation is by definition unfortunate. Who says "That bill got paid," or "Those car keys got found."

Intelligent children recognize that this "it happened" technique can be useful to them too.

When a parent says sternly, "How did that vase get broken?" a sound answer is, "It dropped." This is factually correct and commits a child to nothing. As an answer it tends to irritate parents who usually want more explicit information such as "Who dropped it?" This is a more or less inevitable question as any child knows and has to be handled according to the technique that experience with this particular parent and this particular kind of situation has demonstrated to be most effective. That encompasses a fairly wide variation of response. In the meantime there is no doubt that the "it happened" technique has provided a certain insulation in an awkward moment. Properly used it can wear a parent down to the point where he may even decide to give up altogether and, with any luck at all, it will dilute the crisis. There is, of course, the risk that a parent might detect a reminiscent familiarity in the technique and become highly indignant at such blatant plagiarism, but risks are an inevitable part of living.

The effectiveness of this simple device has a direct correlation with the long stream of things that just go wrong. Tricycles sit obstinately on sidewalks, cups fall from tables, toys get broken and games get lost. One little girl of my acquaintance after a burst of generosity that divided a fresh batch of cookies among her hungry friends, explained to her mother with superb aplomb, "They got eaten." It was an indisputable fact. The sheer starkness of the statement left her mother speechless. There is a reasonable probability that it was out of experiences like this that elves and gremlins were first invented and have to this day continued their nefarious activities and beneficent purposes.

There are other convenient devices to which language can be manipulated. Some adults are fond of occupying that sheltered slot of sentence structure known as the object of the active verb. There is a world of difference, for example, between the version, "That Cadillac hit me," and its opposite number, "I hit that Cadillac." Not only do unhappy situations just happen when one is in the general vicinity, but they even take careful aim and alight on one's innocent head. That plaintive question, "Why does everything have to happen to me?" is an enduring human complaint to which no one expects or wants an answer. Any answer might turn up the fact that what happened was given a neat push by one's own hand. That is clearly no answer.

Inanimate objects as well as other humans do all kinds of unpleasant things to bring trouble down upon one's defenseless head. Baby crawls under the table, straightens up too soon and bangs his head. He stares at the offending table with a wary eye, and a sympathetic adult contributes to the general confusion by insisting, "That bad old table banged baby's head. We'll just hit it." The small one figures that is correct. The table certainly hit him and it hurt. He is, however, sensibly suspicious of the efficacy of that adult slap and the next time he backs half way across the room before he cautiously raises his head too high.

Every adult knows that inanimate objects can continue their unjustified persecution all through life. There are gadgets that will work like dolls for some people and give up immediately when confronted by others. What they do to people they dislike has no limits. While an occasional person admits a lurking suspicion that he might have something to do with the sad results, he doesn't usually pursue this too far. That might land him into a sentence like, "I can't make gadgets work," and there he is occupying the front seat of that insidious grammatical construction, exposed to all the hazards of that dangerous little pronoun "I."

Naturally the situation is somewhat different when other people are the ones precipitating the unfortunate circumstances. There has to be some attempt at explaining why they began the whole business, and this can get quite involved. Not only does the other guy start the trouble, but his reasons cannot have a solid leg to stand on. The victim of his activities can have nothing to do with his obscure motivations, and any explanations are going to have to come from someplace else. The advantage of "what she did to me," over "what I did to her," are perfectly clear. Furthermore, the reasons why "she did to me what she did do," are her problem, not mine.

This linguistic geography is not lost on children. It is usually the kid next door who starts all the fights. Our small hero was playing quietly at home, minding his own business until that budding delinquent next door attacked him without reason and practically demanded that he retaliate. Brothers and sisters are indispensable resources for this purpose. Any parent who ever tried to unravel the mystery of who started the current fracas knows that the one certainty is that the next kid in line is the guilty party. This can go on indefinitely and pursued to its illogical conclusion can contribute dangerously to parental blood pressure.

While children are quite capable of learning such useful techniques on their own initiative, there is no question that adult examples are a considerable help in illuminating their usefulness. For instance, grownups in complaining how all this happened to them often acquire a tone of aggrieved self-righteousness that enhances the dramatic impact of the unfortunate event. Children imitate this tonal inflection with fidelity and find that it improves the feel of authenticity in their recital. This kind of imitation can be excessively irritating to grownups who weren't even aware of their own vocal pitch until they heard it coming back at them.

All of these devices have one primary purpose, to take the one in question off the spot where he can be held responsible for his own behavior. It is not a particularly noble objective but it is a very human one. It is difficult for even grownups to take direct and undisguised responsibility for their own mistakes. For children it is much harder. They even have to learn that this is desirable behavior not to mention the risks they expose themselves to. They have to learn in addition what adults consider mistakes. These may turn out to be activities that seem highly desirable to children such as painting pictures on the wall with Mother's lipstick. Adult reactions become the criteria for what is a mistake, but those reactions do not necessarily make much sense to the children.

They prefer whenever possible to avoid parental wrath and disapproval, and, at the same time, they have a strong yen to engage in any number of actions that parents regard as definitely undesirable. A device such as the "it happened to me," is a neat way of trying to have it both ways even if its success is not always total. In time children may learn more subtle ways of handling this dilemma which go beyond even the remarkable facility of language.

One very bright three-year-old had already worked out one of the most efficacious of these techniques. Her problem was that her parents objected strenuously to her insistent tormenting of the family cat. She had a personal vendetta with that cat of long duration. Almost her first articulate sentence had been "bite kitty" and she did. She also pulled his tail, hauled him around by a firm grip on his throat and in general made life a perpetual hazard for that unhappy animal. Not even his frantic retaliation in the form of frequent scratches deterred her. Just why she had conceived so relentless an antipathy for the cat, who seemed an inoffensive enough creature, never became clear. Her parents had stopped inquiring into the why and concentrated on stopping the all too clear existence of the what.

They made some headway against this steady persecution and began to hope the worst was over. One afternoon the little girl settled down beside me to talk about this and that. The cat who had been asleep beside me opened an eye and regarded his enemy warily. Apparently deciding that my presence constituted sufficient protection he went back to sleep. Presently, in the course of conversation my small friend got around to the subject of the cat.

Reaching over to stroke him gently she observed, "I'm good to the kitty. I pet him like this. I never hurt him. But my sister is mean to him." Looking at me with righteous and sincere indignation she added, "My sister pulls his tail—just like this." With the emphasis of the last three words she suited the action to the thought. The cat, not being properly informed as to the complicated nature of her action, gave a frantic yell and leaped for safety. His small tormentor caught him in midair with a firm grasp around his throat, plunked him unceremoniously onto the couch beside her and without releasing her stranglehold began to stroke him softly with the free hand.

She smiled serenely at me and added, "But I don't do that. I'm good to the kitty. I pet him like this."

"But who," I asked, "just pulled his tail?"

The little girl gave me a cold blank stare and announced that she had to go and see if Carol, her favorite doll, had waked up from her nap. There are times when children can be really frightening.

That small girl had already stumbled upon the perfect solution for doing what you want while at the same time making it perfectly clear that you're not doing it at all because someone else is. It's a relatively simple sleight-of-hand trick although its more ambitious applications require some tortuous elaborations and considerable skill. Accuse someone else— preferably someone weaker or out of sight—of engaging in the particular variety of reprehensible behavior desired (it's always by definition reprehensible), yell loudly enough to focus the audience's attention upon that chosen victim, and while everyone is looking in the wrong direction, you're the one actually behaving that way. It's a trick that works very well with many adults.

Of course, my small friend is still crude and obvious in her implementation of it, but she hasn't had much experience yet. Also she's still handicapped by the fact that she knows perfectly well what she's doing. In a few years she can begin to approach the smoothness of adults who are completely convinced that they never wanted to pull the cat's tail, are not doing so now, and are, as a result, free to be very angry at sister who did do such a heinous action.

In its finished state this device is an indispensable ingredient of such adult interests as favorite prejudices. There was the woman who said blandly, "All Jews cheat," and who was at the time trying with considerable subtlety to finagle an em-

ployee out of an agreed upon raise in pay. If one had asked
her, "And who is doing the cheating?" she would have been
more sophisticated than my little friend but the end result
would have been much the same. At least the children don't
kid themselves nor do they try to take on those global abstractions, all of anything. The little girl was satisfied with
one sister. She hadn't become so ambitious that she had to
have all sisters.

Sex Is Here
to Stay

SEX HAS been a matter of considerable interest to humanity for quite a long time. At various periods of history it has been considered chiefly if not solely an adult prerogative, and children were expected to be ignorant, innocent and disinterested. It is dubious that children ever shared this idea although they certainly learned to be discreet. They also learned that grownups could be shocked at some of, to a child, the most unexpected moments.

The young begin with the naive idea that sex is simply one of the more interesting and pleasant aspects of an interesting and pleasant anatomy. They are distinctly proud of that anatomy and are happy to display it in its full unclothed beauty upon the slightest provocation or no provocation at all. More than one parent has looked up from the graceful amenities of an adult get-together of an evening to see two-year-old Johnny presenting himself for the admiration of the guests with the proud nudity of a Greek statue. This elicits rather mixed reactions in grownups who don't know whether they're amused, embarrassed or envious, but are, in any case, pretty sure that this blatant pleasure in such obvious display cannot continue unchecked. A pretty dress or a handsome new suit could be tactfully admired without prolonging the focus of attention to the point of absurdity, but what does one do when the young ask that their glowing admiration for their own figures be shared. Adults are, of course, used to admiring figures but under more carefully controlled circumstances. For parents, the situation may be further complicated by an uneasy question of what the guests may be thinking.

In sophisticated circles they should, by all the rules, be thinking practically nothing at all. The trouble is one never knows whether such sophistication is genuine or merely fashionable. There was indeed a period not so long ago when *avant garde* parents in the name of the new sexual freedom even ran the children competition in an intellectual, self-conscious sort of way. Anything more devastating to the normal, happy curiosity of children could scarcely be devised by the confused convolutions of the adult mind. It is precisely the unabashed happiness of the young in their new discovery of sexual pleasure that discommodes grownups. They can understand sex, as a problem, a vice, a cause, a power, even a sanctity, but to regard it simply as fun leaves them baffled and distinctly uneasy. It's like hearing someone yell out a four-letter word in the middle of a church service.

What rarely seems to occur to adults is that they and the young are talking about two quite different matters. They are related, unquestionably, but then so is drinking milk from a bottle and eating sirloin steak. Nobody assumes that because they both satisfy hunger they are therefore identical. Grownups are always and forever falling into that ancient trap that children somehow must incorporate adult emotion and desires in their small bodies or else have none at all. It is one of those human blind spots that costs everyone dear.

Until the complications of the adult world trip them up, the young go merrily along enjoying the pleasant sensations of eating what they like, relieving themselves when they like and indulging in a little sexual pleasure when it occurs to them. None of this lasts for long. Like everyone else they have to learn about balanced diets, the rules of hygiene and the requirements of civilization. One young man, protesting the necessity of interrupting his play to go to the bathroom, observed indignantly, "The dogs do it outside. Why can't I?" Because he's not a dog—that's why. There's no use pretending that civilization is an unmitigated joy to the young. But then, even for grownups it has its problems now and then. The point is there's no use in expecting the young to grow up over night, or in assuming that they're going to feel the same way as grownups, let alone understand the adult point of view.

Small children are curious about sex as they are about most things in their world. They investigate with scientific thoroughness, given the opportunity, how other small ones are made, and they definitely enjoy a little mutual experimentation. The fact that males and females are differently constituted is less an incitement to what adults refer to as sexual play than a question of how come. Since the young are much impressed by the visible and the tangible, this is a question of no small importance.

One three-year-old boy, having just made this rather basic discovery, queried his mother at some length about the whole matter. Were all little boys made like him? Did that definitely

include Bill and Dick and John? Were no little girls blessed
with that convenient appendage? Finally convinced, he observed with a deep sigh of relief, "My, I'm glad I've got one."
While the gods were distributing favors, he was very glad
he'd been in the right line. His sister got even with him later
by making it very clear that only girls can have babies. She
was not exactly sure how or why this was so, but there was
no doubt that it was so. This was somewhat disturbing to the
small proud male because children consider babies as very important indeed. However, the young like everyone else have
to learn sometime that no one can have everything in this
world. At that, small brother still held the advantage. Maybe
it was true only girls could have babies, but he didn't see sister
having any. He might even settle for a compromise such as
the one a young man once carefully explained to me. The
ladies go to the hospital and bring back girl babies, he explained, while fathers go to the hospital and bring back boy
babies. Time will certainly disabuse him of that ingenious fantasy, but in the meantime it makes life very difficult for sister.
The words are there, but the evidence is not immediately
available.

Grownups regard all this childish confusion with the tolerant amusement of superior knowledge. The idea that a
woman is an incomplete man certainly has no place in a scientific age even if it has caused plenty of trouble in less enlightened times. By and large, adults are less amused by the
youthful curiosity that brought the whole matter up in the
first place. There is an uneasy feeling that sex becomes altogether too real among the young and who knows what iniqui-
ties may not result. They are much safer playing adult cha-
rades and being proper little girl friends and boy friends. The

young soon get the idea. If they want to pursue any more scientific researches, they'd better stay out of sight and remember to watch their tongues afterward. When they're old enough to have the proper vocabulary and the proper detachment, they can talk as much as they like. The talking seems, oddly enough, to become more important in the modern climate of sexual freedom.

Grownups are caught up in the confusion of conflicting ideas and standards, and no one is very clear just where it should all end. On TV they watch a four-year-old being interviewed about his girl friend and prospective plans for matrimony. They are properly aghast when he introduces the prospect at age sixteen. They are warned that any girl who reaches puberty without at least one reliably present boy friend may be doomed to a life of lonely spinsterhood, not to mention social ostracism for the turbulent teens. They are also appalled by the consequences of early marriage not to mention illegitimate offspring. Everyone is positive sex is the one sure-fire way to sell anything from books to soap, but children should show some sense and forget about it until they're old enough to support a family. They ought to be able to concentrate on the soap and leave the rest to their elders.

Furthermore, they should be sufficiently intelligent to listen to what grownups say, and stop peeking around corners to observe with deadly concentration what the grownups do. The behavior of adults in this interesting area of human activity has a distinct propensity for deviation from the type of behavior verbally approved by those same adults. This is actually a venerable phenomenon which in the past was pretty well understood as a matter of preserving appearances and a reasonable amount of order. That did in effect set certain limits beyond which only the most reckless would venture and it also had a tendency to limit opportunity for some of humanity's rasher impulses. It took the twentieth century to come up with a combination of vastly expanded opportunities and the idea that people should believe what they said on the subject of sexual morality and act accordingly. Since adults had rarely been confronted before with the question of what they believed, this has caused a great deal of turmoil. About the only consensus has been that children should confine their interest in sex to TV interviews and school hygiene classes until they're old enough to find out what, if anything, they believe. There is even a wistful half-concealed hope that they might come up with a solution that could be relayed to their elders.

In the meantime parents debate apprehensively about how often Johnny should tear off in the family car, how late Mary should stay out with her boy friend and what to do about teen-age parties that last all night. Legislatures battle over the age when the young should be given license to drive and to drink. Everybody is convinced moral deterioration has set in, that the consequences are deplorable and that something should be done about it. Almost nobody agrees on what precisely that something is or who should do it.

This does not mean that grownups have done nothing about the situation. On the contrary, they have managed to introduce one of the cleverest and most subtle ideas that the fertile imagination of man has come up with in some time. They decided to desexualize sex. Only the astonishing intelligence of Homo sapiens could have conceived an idea so fundamentally simple and far-reaching. Insist that sex is a social game, make the eligibility requirements for admission to that game rigorous enough that all-out effort will be required for any strata worthy of mention, introduce a stiff admixture of competition, exact penalties for failure that will make grownups and young alike quiver with anxiety—and who has time or energy for sex. It's a nice twist on the old idea that sex is real, but should be so carefully attired in public view that no one will be blatantly reminded. Now the appearances of virtue can pretty well be disregarded because sex isn't real and the appearances are about all that is. The whole matter has become practically indistinguishable from an automobile company with a new model coming out every fall nicely decorated with synthetic sex appeal.

Naturally, to make the idea effective there has to be a good deal of preparation and consistent vigilance to see that nobody's mind starts wandering in the wrong directions. There is nothing like early indoctrination to prevent such untoward possibilities. In that perspective the coy questions of adults to the young relative to their matrimonial plans and their current romances are not so absurd as at first glance they appear. Right from the beginning children are to understand that their spontaneous interest in sex as a physiological pleasure simply won't do. Sex is a social game concerned with pairing off with the proper girl or boy friend, going steady, making vague and absurd plans for future marriage and learning the proper social appurtenances of the process. The same grownups who are horrified with the four-year-old's direct methods of learning how other four-year-olds are made, beam with amusement and pride when the four-year-old gentleman presents his small girl friend with a bouquet of flowers or the offer of a chocolate soda. Crude sex has been neatly disguised with the pretty flounces of a romantic tableau, and there is a nebulous feeling that maybe it has gone away.

By the time the young are well into grammar school, they are already experts at the intricate steps and stylized flourishes of the great game. The pairing of male and female must be accomplished in faithful imitation of the latest adult techniques and with as much aplomb as can be mustered at that immature age. Naturally all such pairings must occur in public view. That is, after all, the main purpose of the game. Keep sex in the open, properly attired and suitably decorated, and nobody has to worry about it except, possibly, the young themselves. This everything-in-the-open approach has all kinds of useful consequences.

It gives adults a fine modern impression of having finally escaped the musty prudery of the puritanical past. Everyone, even children, can talk about sex—no more hushed half-sentences and garbled innuendoes. If a child wants to know where babies come from, he doesn't have to settle for any peripatetic storks. He can have a scientific lecture instead. It may leave him a little befuddled at first, but at least he can have no question of the eminent discussability of sex. In fact, he may even wonder how a simple question landed him in such a rarefied intellectual altitude. Naturally he is too young to realize that by this and other methods sex can be elevated to the level of scholarly and scientific discussion. In other words it can be talked to death. Some of the brighter members of the younger set seem to get an uneasy inkling that some kind of sleight-of-hand is going on, but it takes time and experience to follow the subtleties of the adult mind, and by that time it is usually too late.

The message is, in any case, clear enough. It is perfectly all right to talk about sex. It could even be said that for anyone desiring to be really modern it is incumbent to do so. Discussion has all the advantages of titillation with practically none of the hazards that would otherwise be a usual accompaniment of such a state. It gives the discussants a pleasant consciousness of sophistication spiced with a dash of daring. Best of all, it is all out in the open. Nobody has to pretend that he's really talking about zoology unless he belongs to such an *avant garde* circle that open discussion of sex is regarded as a little outmoded. In either case, the really important point is to stay in style and keep talking. Nobody has unlimited time and energy, and there's nothing like discussion to absorb a goodly hunk of both.

It is obviously important that this message get through to the young by adolescence. On the other hand, it cannot be counted upon by itself to be reliably effective with the members of that impetuous group. There have to be other ways of diverting attention and energies. The social game is equal to the challenge, and the rules are already at work. Popularity is the true goal. Once involved in that struggle it is practically impossible to concentrate on anything else, and, of course, popularity must take place in public view or there is no point to it at all.

The whole fun of achieving so desirable a state depends upon a wide and numerous audience. Without that, the lucky girl whose engagement book is full to the covers with a plethora of suitable young men would be reduced to considering how much she actually enjoyed the company of each. With an admiring and envious gallery of spectators, that is largely irrelevant. The real point is the over-all effect upon the judgment of the gallery. If the quantity and quality of the young men are up to standard, the accolade is bestowed. The lucky girl is a social and sexual success. This does not mean that she has necessarily had any direct experience with sex. Popularity based on a desperate promiscuity is subject to scorn and disqualifies the offender for the true contest. Sex, of course, has little more than a peripheral relevance since it is the ego rather than the heart that is at stake, but there can be no question of the practicality of the rules.

Winners in the popularity race, like winners in any race, simply cannot exist without losers, and the losers by definition must outnumber the winners. While the race itself can absorb almost unlimited time and attention, there have to be alternative solutions. The first consideration is to be in the game, and that means pairing off with proper public recognition. Going steady is a kind of social insurance. Both members of the partnership are protected from that most dreaded of fates— exclusion from the social circle. Under the threat of that fate individual choice of a partner is fine when possible, but scarcely of primary consideration. Of course, even necessity can be dressed up with the furbelows of romance and can make a rather pretty picture for the casual eye. Adults are a little uneasy when personal choice and continuous proximity are allied. That's the trouble with sex. It keeps reverting to its natural state with so little regard for social games, let alone long-range consequences.

With all the complex and tortuous efforts, there is no use pretending the results are an unqualified success. It is cold comfort to reflect that no age with any pretensions to sophistication has come up with the perfect answer of what to do about people and sex. We have to live in this age, and the confusion seems to grow worse rather than better. Whatever solution the ingenious human race finally evolves, there is a good likelihood that for happiness it will have to find some way to combine the spontaneous wisdom of the young with the self-discipline of maturity.

The young left to themselves reserve their love-making exclusively for those people they like very much. That means grownups mostly. With their compatriots they may be curious, but they don't often devote much serious attention to each other. Uncomplicated by the ulterior uses of seduction that will occur to them later, they bring a wholehearted, whole-bodied zest to enamoring the person of their choice. Their concern is how they can win a reciprocating devotion. This zest can create certain problems for the grownup since children are not particularly subtle and are prone to permit the realities of sex to become visible through the delicate veil of romance. Just how one restrains this youthful ardor without offending the delightful small person who feels it is one of those questions that tax the ingenuity and art of the most sensitive adult. The vulnerability of the young to a so-beloved grownup is one of the most touching, lovely and delicate feelings in all the lexicon of human emotion.

To the very young sex is real, uncomplicated, spontaneous and fun, but distinctly different from what adults mean and feel by it. Nature has a sensible way of adapting the emotions and their expression to the physiology. There is nothing unusual in the behavior of a two-year-old who expressed his fervent admiration for an adult friend of mine by proudly urinating in her presence. She was one of those rare grownups who understood that this was a compliment, and her small friend felt very good about the whole matter. His sister, aged four, took a rather more jaundiced view and remarked in faithful imitation of adult world-weariness, "Aren't men awful?" The adult who expressed admiration in such a fashion would properly find himself in the psychiatric ward of the nearest hospital.

Children are just plain elemental and there's no use pretending sex is either a social game or an academic subject for them. They have a lot to learn before they can achieve the confusion and sophistication of the adult world, and a lot of growing to do before sex becomes as dangerous as grownups have a shrewd suspicion it can be. In the meantime, children are unquestionably the most discouraging sign that sex is going to survive the most arduous education and continue to bring trouble, excitement and, now and then, a surprising zest for life and love to the bewildered human race.

The Young
Have Dignity Too

THE WORD dignity is one frequently to be heard these days. Democracy stands for human dignity; totalitarianism destroys it. It is rather amazing, considering how much we talk about it, that we seem to confine its value so much to humans of grown size. The smaller the person, the less we worry about his dignity. Sometimes we even find the idea a little ludicrous as if smallness and inexperience were incompatible with anything so majestic as human dignity.

While we don't exactly phrase it that way, we assume that dignity goes with suitable clothes, proper manners and the occasional sonorous phrase. Or it resembles Michelangelo's "Moses" and is tremendous, powerful, invulnerable. Neither picture seems to have much connection with Billy making mudpies in the backyard. Yet children have a great sense of their own dignity. They couldn't define what it is but they know when it has been violated. They can react to those violations with an intensity that convinces their elders that children simply don't make any sense. Adults rarely stop to consider how they react to affronts to their own dignity and still more rarely see that the situations are in any sense comparable. In consequence, children learn early that most grownups have very delicate sensibilities that should be tip-toed around without a jar while their own may be trampled on with impunity. It is quite probable that the delicacy of adult sensibilities is a direct result of the beating they took when these adults were themselves small.

Take the everyday hazards any attractive two- or three-year-old is exposed to when he walks down the street with his proud mother. Like any human he enjoys being admired by the passers-by, but like any self-respecting human he appreciates some restraint in the expression of that admiration. Instead he is patted, pinched, even kissed and picked up by perfect strangers who coo at him in upper-register tones that make his eardrums wince. Even this wouldn't be so bad if he could pick his admirers. There are people one enjoys being kissed by even at age two and then there are people where one prefers to keep a certain distance. Choice is just what the two-year-old doesn't have. Unless Mother comes to the rescue, the tall strangers do all the choosing.

One mother told me quite seriously that she had quite a problem with her small daughter. The little girl was extremely pretty, and strangers in the street were forever stopping to pat or kiss her or pick her up. At that point she kicked them. This is clearly a healthy, self-respecting response. It may be a problem to the strangers on the street, but one can only observe that they asked for it. The little girl handled the situation very competently considering the limited resources at her disposal. Verbal protests are usually ineffective, as she had probably learned from experience because a firm "No" only results in such unanswerable questions as "What's the matter, darling? You're such a beautiful little girl. Why won't you give me a smile?" A firm kick, on the other hand, usually brings the whole affair to a quick and decisive conclusion. It may be somewhat of a problem for Mother, torn between pride in her daughter's admirable qualities and apprehension at the ensuing contretemps, but there's no use asking a child to take on the adult's problems.

The whole matter falls into proper perspective if one imagines a strange adult on the street behaving in so impetuous a manner toward another adult. The object of such unsolicited admiration would promptly call the police. The difference is that the adult is treated as a person while the child is regarded as a charming object, something in the nature of a piece of crystal to be tapped to see if it rings. This is such an obvious violation of human dignity that the wonder is not that a few children revolt, but that so many resign themselves to tacit endurance. I suppose they accept it as one more evidence of adult irrationality which can never be understood by a sensible child.

I once saw a doting grandmother push this particular brand of nonsense to even greater lengths. She came to call with her three-year-old granddaughter on friends who had a three-year-old boy. The two children who had not met before looked each other over with the wary curiosity of two strange dogs. The adults promptly intervened with the usual admonitions about making friends and what a lovely little boy and girl each certainly was. The children ignored this. They'd heard it all before and were aware that it had less than nothing to do with the reality. They were just beginning to make

a few cautious overtures toward each other when Grandmother had a bright idea.

"Janey, kiss the little boy. He's such a nice little boy and I
know he'd like a big kiss from you," she bubbled cheerfully.

Janey's face set in mutinous lines and her response was a
succinct, "No." The "nice" little boy looked surprised,
bewildered and uneasy. He'd already been around long
enough to know that this situation boded no good for anyone.
Grandmother persisted, at first cheerfully, then with growing
irritation and finally with grim determination that had lost all
sight of the original suggestion. Janey had guts and stubbornness, and she held out until her tenacity promised to result in
physical violence. By that time both children were in tears.
She finally gave the little boy a brief peck on the cheek, but
not even the most obtuse adult could have mistaken that
gesture for affection.

While the little boy's mother had taken no part in this
compulsory osculation, neither had she stepped in and put a
stop to the ridiculous situation. She was neatly tethered by
those rules which insist that it is much safer to offend the
children than other grownups. Nor was the grandmother a
heinous monster. She had had the impulsive idea that it would
be "cute" to see Janey kiss her small compatriot, and it would
make a pretty story to relate to the neighbors later, with her
part in it expurgated, naturally. When the idea ran headlong
into a stone wall, she was caught in the presence of another
adult with a flat challenge to her authority. With grim
humorlessness she thought she had to meet the challenge
head-on, and after that the end was predictable. What the
grownups overlooked completely was their affront to the
children's dignity.

It was strictly the children's business whether they kissed or didn't. If they had, which was highly unlikely, they would have done so because they felt like it, not as a stage performance for the amusement of an impromptu audience. Any self-respecting person who treasures his own dignity has the same feeling. He likes to choose the recipients of his affectionate gestures, and he does not appreciate being pushed around like an animated doll. It is even possible that from lessons like this comes the first training in that dubious art of using the symbols of affection as a lockpick for the advantages one is currently seeking. It is a pity the most civilized of emotions can be subverted to the crudest of ends.

As a matter of fact, cuteness in children is totally an adult perspective. The children themselves are unaware that the quality exists, let alone its desirability, until the reactions of grownups inform them. They cannot, by definition, recognize that incongruity of words and actions that are the essence of their elders' delight. Unfortunately the laughter of adults too often carries to the ears of the young the ring of ridicule, that annihilating enemy of human dignity. Like grownups, children enjoy participating in a joke and appreciate admiration of their wit and cleverness, but do not enjoy being the butt of the jokes.

I remember a baby scarcely beyond his first birthday who lost in an effort to stand with proud independence and fell with aplomb upon a pillow. The grownups laughed because the way he fell and the indignant expression upon his face were funny. The baby stared at them and then his small face crumpled and tears filled his eyes. He had not minded the fall. That was a part of the serious business of learning to live and move upright. He did mind the laughter which reduced the reality of his efforts to the indignity of the merely amusing.

Only gradually do children learn that there are practical advantages to be won from the strange citizens of this strange world of the grownups by playing the game deliberately. If they laugh at a mispronounced word, say it again and keep them laughing. If they find a confusion of meaning uproarious—like a small friend of mine who asked if we had tilted the waitress—repeat the mistake. Learn to say and do those little things which adults find so enticing and then collect. Not even this works for long, of course. There's no way of being at once calculating and spontaneous short of a genius for acting, and with calculation the grownups stop laughing. Now they say with irritation, "Johnny, stop being so silly."

The spontaneous reaction of most healthy children to that parental plea, "Tell Aunt Mary and Uncle Joe how you say 'interrupt' " is a clear and succinct "No." It is a reaction they should not surrender. No matter how irritated adults may be, it is the only sure way of defending their innate dignity as people. It is interesting that to the end of our days most of us find the gently patronizing laugh and the harsh sting of ridicule the most devastating attack of all upon the essential dignity of personality.

The sense of personal dignity comes with the dawning awareness that one is a separate individual. The baby sees himself only as he is reflected in the eyes of others. He has to explore his own body to know what is there. He views his toes with the same surprised delight as a four-year-old disemboweling a clock. There is even the same objective detachment and dispassionate concentration. When he masters the first intricacies of speech, he refers to himself by name or by the third person pronoun because that is the way other people refer to him. He is still the faithful little mirror.

He says, "Give Billy a cookie" or "Billy doesn't want to go to bed." Adults often have a propensity for imitating this pattern of speech. Mother says cheerfully, "Mother wants Billy to go to bed now" or "Does Billy want a cookie?" This sort of thing adds to the general confusion and is clearly reminiscent of the parrot and "Polly wants a cracker." A child wants or doesn't want, feels one way or another, but he doesn't recognize himself. Like the puppy who barks at his reflection in the mirror, he is not yet conscious that he is someone who can project an image.

As all parents know, the next pronoun to make its ubiquitous appearance is the possessive "mine." Long before the small one has arrived at consciousness of himself as a separate and distinct individual, he has acquired a proprietary concern with certain recognizable objects. The basis of his claim may frequently be questionable, but there is no doubt of his conviction. One small girl shopping with her mother spotted one of those intriguing dolls that drinks from a bottle and duly wets its pants. While her mother was occupied, she quietly abducted the doll, filled the small bottle at a nearby water fountain and was well into the engrossing business of feeding said doll before she was discovered.

When her mother attempted to rectify the situation, the little girl clung to the doll screaming indignantly, "Mine, mine." No amount of explanation shook her conviction that the doll was hers because she had claimed it first. The intensity of that conviction finds certain echoes in the grownup world. At least where children are concerned, there can be no argument about that proverbial bird in hand, and its tag is marked "mine."

With time children graduate from the third person pronoun to a closer recognition of consciousness as persons—

though without relinquishing that insistent possessive "mine." Now Billy says, "Me wants a cookie" or "Me doesn't want to go to bed." That is not just a matter of erroneous grammar. He still sees himself as me, the object, not I, the doer. In fact, when he is unhappy he can cling to that state of me, the object, as if it were a refuge.

One young father became aware that his son, Philip, was continuing to refer to himself in this fashion long after he should have taken that momentous step to the first person pronoun. The parents were well educated and Philip heard correct grammar. What he didn't hear was enough attention to justify an importance that would warrant such a step. He had an older brother who had the advantage of seniority and a small sister who had the dual advantage of femininity and infancy. In the inevitable hurly-burly of caring for three children neither parent had noticed that Phil was a bit of an also-ran. Since they didn't give him the importance of a tall "I," he didn't give himself that importance either. He stayed with the short, babyish "me." When his parents observed this, they began stressing the advantage of being Philip and making it worth his while. Within weeks he was proudly saying, "I want a cookie" and "I don't want to go to bed."

To the harassed parent that can seem a small advantage. The kid still wants a cookie and still doesn't want to go to bed. When your feet hurt and your head aches, that can seem the more relevant consideration. Yet that long step from "me" to "I" is one of the most important a human being ever takes. With it comes the first consciousness of identity, the first inkling of responsibility, the first awareness of the importance of personal dignity. It is the first step on a long road he will travel until death sets the final block.

Probably very few travel it all the way, and some people turn off early. There are those who always try to settle for "it happened to me," rather than "I did." There are those who get as far as "I want," but never make it to "I give." There are those for whom "I" remains pretty much a reflection of what other people think and approve, an "I" that never grew strong enough to stand on its own roots. For them that "I" may remain so wobbly that in their own thoughts it is translated back to that impersonal third person "he" or "she" as an insulation from the open winds of responsibility and individuality. Perhaps nearly everyone lapses at times into those strange self-conversations that split "I" into two people, one obviously a ghost, and that begin "You should have known." Just who is talking to whom and which one is "I" is not often questioned. The road to self-completion is a long one and a hard one, and the first wavering step on its rough surface remains a great occasion in the momentous history of a life.

The young, of course, like *nouveaux riches*, have a tendency to overdo a good thing. They have a definite feeling that the newly glimpsed identity is entitled to some measure of recognition. With this they begin to say "No" to everything, right and left. "Johnny, pick up your toys."

"No."

"Johnny, get ready for dinner."

"No."

It is a kind of negative declaration of independence. Since Johnny doesn't have much idea what it is he wants to be independent of, he settles more or less for a blanket "No." Once in a while he even trips himself up and says "No" to an offer of an ice cream cone, before he catches himself and rectifies the mistake. The general idea seems to run something like this.

"I may be small and I may be weak, but I'm a person and just because you're big, don't get the idea you can push me around." The ubiquitous "No" is a defense system always on alert with a definite tendency to regard all bystanders, particularly bigger ones, as potential encroachers on the new citadel.

Of all the qualities of the young which irritate their elders, this one easily ranks near the top. That consistent "No" has something of the same effect as the Chinese water torture. It drips away at adult patience with a steady monotony that can upon occasion bring the most solid parent to the screaming point. Some grownups try sweet reason and have even been known to ask, "Why don't you want to pick up your toys?" This is an approach that rarely endures long and has a practically perfect record of failure. Other adults get angry at the very idea of a person so small saying "No" to a person so big. They call it impertinence, plus quite a few other colloquial descriptions that add up to, "Just who does he think he is." Adults like these rarely notice that they don't think he is anyone entitled to any ideas of his own. Even more rarely do they notice any inconsistency when they admire the little guy who stands up to the big guy in the grownup world. When you put the whole matter into perspective, it does take a good bit of courage and plenty of stubbornness for someone as small as a two-year-old to say "No" to someone more than twice his size. The convenient adult idea that he knows nothing worse than a slap can happen to him has little but convenience to recommend it.

The answer to the whole problem rests with a little everyday observation and a modicum of endurance. Any parent who ignores the "No" soon learns that nine times out of ten the small rebel having registered his protest goes ahead and does what was asked of him. He never had any serious objection in the first place, but he did feel it incumbent to assert his presence in the world before complying. The sensible parent acknowledges his right to said assertion and expects him to comply with instructions within a reasonable interval after that. There is no question that that interval can be excessively trying at times, but then, waiting for other adults can be trying too. In any case, trying to rush a two-year-old into anything is probably the most futile expenditure of energy any adult can attempt. The more big people respect the dignity of little people the less trouble they have with the compliance of the young.

Who doesn't resent being ordered about as if he were a robot that only needed to be wound up and commanded? A good deal of youthful defiance is directed less toward the nature of the command than the way it is expressed. I remember one intelligent little boy who habitually fought his father with a grim tenacity worthy of a better cause. If his father said "No," he said "Yes," and vice versa. He usually lost the battle because the odds were all on his father's side, but the next day he was back in the war. What he was fighting was not his father's orders but his father's refusal to grant him the dignity of a person. He wanted something as simple as a "Please," as fundamental as a right to an opinion of his own, as decent as acceptance of inevitable mistakes without mockery.

Like all children he wanted the quiet acknowledgment of importance that courtesy bestows upon its recipients. This does not imply some elaborate artificial formality that seeks the right words for its channels. It is the courtesy of the heart that respects the importance of another no matter how small he is, and therefore does not humiliate him, however casually. It finds no conflict with authority because the truly courteous do not give orders to display their own power to do so. It offers leeway to the young, recognizing they have their own areas of decision that need not and should not be usurped by their elders. It does not find it dangerous or debasing to acknowledge that big people as well as little people can be wrong at times, can make mistakes and can be sorry.

Most of all, children want respect for their emotions, however incongruous, unreasonable or even ridiculous these may seem to adults. The cavalier attitude that assumes the feelings of the small may be disregarded while those of the grownups are sacrosanct strikes at the soul of human dignity. What a child fears may seem nonsense to the adult, but his fear is no less real.

I remember a little boy who asked me to walk him home although the distance was short because it was after dark and he must pass an empty lot. On the way he asked with considerable hesitation if I could supply some reason for my presence so his parents need not know he had been afraid. He was afraid of the dark streets because they were peopled with the ghosts of his imagination, but he was more afraid of adult laughter at those ghosts. His fears were not allowed the dignity of respect because in adult eyes they had no reality. Yet adults have their own ghosts, and they fear those ghosts, and they've been known to insist they are real when it is clear they are not. Perhaps their laughter at the young is a cruel and futile rite of exorcism, a meaningless sacrifice to dark and unknown gods. The little boy had an honesty and courage greater than that of his elders. He did not even insist his ghosts must be real for everyone. He simply said he was afraid.

The emotions of children often seem unreasonable or exaggerated to grownups. A child can be wildly angry because Father says, "No, you can't go to the drugstore with me," or he can weep noisily and copiously because Mother says, "No, you can't stay up and join the company tonight." Adults have their own pressures and problems, and the emotions of one small human can seem just what they don't need at that moment. They forget that they can blow up over a triviality and correctly observe, "The plumber didn't show up and that was the last straw." They are describing an accumulation of frustrations and demands, and the last one tipped the scale. That the same thing can happen to the young seems less real because the frustrations and pressures of the young are usually different in nature if not in impact.

Yet a frustration is a frustration, and a demand is a demand. What is immediately relevant is not how reasonable or unreasonable it looks to the cool eyes of an observer, but how it feels to the one involved. The emotion is real whether its source looks justified or otherwise. Respect for that reality is the longing of human dignity. Neither justification nor concession are any necessary part of that respect. The grownup may continue to insist upon the validity of his demand without contradiction of his respect for the emotions it precipitates. The demand may be just or unjust depending upon whose standard it is measured against, but that is a different question.

Dignity is respect for what one is, feels and thinks. It does not insist one is always right nor even necessarily justified. It does not compare one with others for better or for worse because that is truly irrelevant. At heart, dignity is self-honesty and self-respect not self-satisfaction nor self-aggrandizement.

Right to Privacy

EVERY CHILD needs something to hide. There has to be a part of himself, a fantasy, a feeling, an idea, a belief, that is uniquely his own, protected from trespassers and guarded from interlopers. It is not, as adults too readily assume, a guilty secret that he dare not share but a cherished secret that may be offered but not taken. It is, in fact, the keystone of his individuality, the heart of his dignity as a person, his right to privacy.

Without privacy there is no true individuality. There are only types. Individual personality is a process of growth, not a discovery, not a product stamped out by the machine. For that process solitude is as necessary as companionship, quiet as important as activity. Who can know what he thinks and feels if he never has the opportunity to be alone with his thoughts and his feelings. Who can dream of great achievements, of new and wonderful ideas if he never possesses the serene and effortless moments for dreaming. To lie on the ground on a warm, summer afternoon and watch the clouds form and re-form their magic symbols, drift in their orderly calm across a summer sky, to follow the soar and dip of birds, to study the intricate pattern of leaves against the endless expanse of horizon—this is an experience of childhood to be cherished forever.

In our ceaseless endeavor for group experiences, for organized activities we may too easily forget the great experiences of solitude. The longing to create something expressive of one's self may strike sparks from the contact of other people, but its roots grow in privacy. The sudden observation that transforms the taken-for-granted into a new revelation is the outward flash of inner awareness that grows in quiet. There are times when it is more important to communicate with one's self than with others. In fact, how does anyone communicate with another human being if he cannot catch some glimpse of his own soul. One of the strengths and joys of reading is that it is solitary, and so there is room for silent communication with the thoughts and fantasies of another human being. In contrast, the noisy and ubiquitous clatter of the TV offers rare chance for that silent language.

Children are peculiarly vulnerable to invasion of privacy, especially by grownups. For one thing, their elders often forget or ignore that they have any need for it. Yet they show early in life its importance to them. A little child plays quietly, carrying on an animated conversation with a doll or a favorite stuffed animal. He discusses all kinds of things with himself, sometimes happy events, sometimes troublesome problems. When adults overhear these conversations, too seldom do they accord the small soliloquist the respect and dignity of privacy. Sometimes they are amused and let him know it. Sometimes they are impatient and crash abruptly into his world. Sometimes they try to participate in that conversation without so much as a passing thought for their rudeness. Elementary good manners would at least wait for an invitation

before intruding upon a private conversation. Whatever the
adult approach, children react to it as an invasion and correctly so. Their sudden, frozen silence is their only defense.
One perceptive listener who did not intrude overheard a little
boy of four arguing with himself.

In a high artificial voice, quite unlike his usual one, he was
saying, "I hate Mommy. She's mean to me. She's not fair."

Then in his normal voice he answered himself. "Oh no,
you don't hate Mommy. You love her. Look at all the nice
things she does for you and how she takes care of you."

The debate of love and hate is one of life's great themes.
It is no less great because the one who struggles so valiantly
with it is four years old. However one may seek to help him
in this human dilemma, one does not crash into the privacy of
his world, shattering his dignity like a broken glass.

Children need a private world for many reasons. When
the big world outside becomes more than usually confusing
and menacing, small people need a refuge, a safe retreat. Fantasies can wreak swift revenge upon offenders, shore up battered vanity, promise fabulous achievements. Quiet can gentle
tearing emotions, sort out bewildering contradictions, even
open a small window for cool reason. It is no part of relevance
whether the stormy emotions are justified or unjustified by
some distant grown-up standard. They need a refuge to
which their small possessor holds the only key.

I remember one small boy whose special retreat was a
pleasant little room near the family kitchen. When he had had
enough of adult demands, he retreated to that room with the
clear understanding he would not be disturbed until he chose
to rejoin the outside world. He left the door open, except
when he was very angry and had to slam something, and en-

joyed the security of familiar voices with the safety of a protected refuge. One wonders where in modern houses there is
space for a private refuge or quiet for private thoughts.

One boy sought that quiet in walking alone. There was a
woods not far away and he liked to walk among the trees
with the comforting crackle of leaves and twigs underfoot.
Only, as he plaintively complained, it was not easy to go
alone.

"I start out of the house, and someone says, 'Where are
you going?' I say, 'I'm going for a walk' and then my sister or
my brother says, 'Wait a minute and I'll go with you.' Only I
don't always want someone to go with me. Sometimes I
want to go alone."

Some of the young, like this sensitive child, have more
need of privacy than others. They must defend their inner
world not only against adults but against other children.
They need the protection of grownups against the cheerfully
oblivious depredations of brothers and sisters who are more
gregarious. Sometimes they are regarded with suspicion and
apprehension. To want to be alone comes to be something like
a confession of secret vice or probable emotional breakdown.
Adults differ too in their need for solitude and what is privacy
for one can be prison for another, but adults have more resources and know more excuses.

Privacy can be more than a refuge, as the boy who liked
to walk alone in the woods knew. It is also a chance to explore, observe and learn without the prying eyes of others or
the check of interference. There is a new world around every
corner when everything is new and strange to eyes not yet
accustomed. Curiosity is young and fierce, and concentration
is suddenly effortless. Adults with considerable reason take a

rather dim view of this. There are realistic dangers that children cannot know. To pick mushrooms and study them is fine. To taste them indiscriminately can be fatal.

There are also dangers to objects cherished by grownups. A curious member of the young can do a rather effective job of demolishing a clock in order to find out what makes it tick. Adults are usually correct in saying, "When a youngster is quiet too long, he's into some mischief." As every parent knows, drawers are full of fascinating surprises to be felt, tasted, taken apart and strewn about by an enterprising three-year-old. In their understandable irritation at havoc discovered grownups overlook an interesting fact. What is mischief to them has also been a remarkably sustained span of concentration, systematic exploration and individual enterprise. Under more sympathetic circumstances these are known as qualities of high value.

It is a pity parents do not quietly fill some accessible drawers and cupboards with a collection of fascinating things that may safely be tasted, taken apart and strewn about. The quiet part is important because children value the freedom of their own enterprise and are suspicious of adult setups that have an unfortunate tendency to resemble soda water without the fizz. The drawers would not, of course, provide any necessary insurance that others less accessible and less desirably researchable would be safe from prying hands. The young like their elders find the forbidden too tantalizing to be ignored indefinitely.

However mixed their motives, children in the pursuit of their interests display remarkable initiative and concentration, and they develop this to a considerable extent in privacy. A friend of mine still remembers the pains she went to in reaching the top drawer of her mother's bureau. In that drawer was kept a fascinating collection of cosmetics. Happily she took out a box of powder, climbed down from the enabling chair and seated herself on the rug which had a pattern of Oriental colors in fanciful shapes. She was delighted with the effect of powder on these patterns and became happily engrossed with what was in effect an abstract painting in powder on an Oriental rug. She remembers this as a fascinating project of exploring shapes and colors and patterns. It is only fair to add that her mother did not share this point of view. Part of the fun was exploring the forbidden, but what held her concentration—to her own undoing—was the same quality that holds the artist to his canvas.

Concentration is always solitary, even in the midst of a crowd, and there is no real achievement without it. Grownups may argue with the activities children choose to concentrate on, but in their exasperation they have an unfortunate tendency to throw out the baby with the bath. There are times when it might be the better part of wisdom to make some quiet adaptations to individual interests and individual enterprise, even to learn from the choices of the young.

There is a privacy of the body, a privacy of the mind and a privacy of the heart. All of them are ill-fortified in the young against the thoughtlessness and insensitivity of their elders. Grownups are busy and pressured and impatient, and often they crash through barriers so fragile as to be almost invisible, without even the awareness that they were ever there. Only the children mark the devastation.

I remember one charming little boy who at age two delighted in conversation with adults. When he had to devote time to his bodily functions, he liked company. He didn't mind sitting on a toilet seat for the requisite period, but he did object to being bored. This was a time for cheerful companionship with someone he enjoyed, and he saw no occasion for privacy. For a year or so the only problem was coaxing an adult to relax and chat. Then one day when he was almost four, he changed his mind. When a grownup offered to keep him company, he quietly refused. "I'd rather be alone," he explained, requesting at the same time that the adult close the door upon departure.

That little boy was fortunate. The grownup left without laughter, protest or insistence upon explanation. Privacy of the body had become important and with it there was a new dignity and gravity, a sense of self-importance. It was still too nebulous for explanation, too fragile for protest, too important for touch, however light. It was the first flower of that self-esteem without which no true identity can grow.

Privacy of the mind is a cherished right for which, in the modern world, even adults must struggle. The right to think as one desires, to speak or not to speak one's thoughts, to believe or not to believe, is one of the truly great rights of any human being. It is no less a one for the human who has spent only a few years in this world. His thoughts may be different, but they are his own. To protect them from prying eyes and curious inquiries he devises a whole arsenal of ambiguities and nebulosities.

"What are you daydreaming about?"

"Nothing."

"What were you talking to the Jones children about?"

"We were just talking."

"What were you and your brother arguing about?"

"We were just arguing." The list is endless and to adults

both frustrating and infuriating. The silence need not conceal conspiracy—though grownups are chronically suspicious—but it is the caution of those who know doors can be forced.

There is even a further hazard. Who knows when all-powerful adults can read one's thoughts with a glance. A young friend of mine, a girl of twelve, was telling me about a recent disappointment to the effect that a certain important young man had displayed a cutting indifference to her tentative indications of interest. I answered her with, "So, of course, you felt there was something very wrong with you."

To my surprise an expression of fear and resentment flashed across her face.

"Of course, you would know that's the way I felt."

"What do you mean?" I asked, astonished.

"You usually know how I feel. I suppose it's easy for you to know what I'm thinking."

She thought I was a mind-reader. When I explained that I had once been her age and most people have had experiences little different from hers, relief brought affection back to our friendship. Who can like someone who walks through closed doors as if they were not there?

The most important feelings we ever know can be shared as gifts, but to steal them is to destroy them. A small girl woke in the night and shivered from the fears and the loneliness of the dark. Quietly she padded to her parents' room and listened to the sound of their breathing that told of peaceful sleep. She hesitated and then without sound she picked up one of her father's slippers and her mother's robe. Cuddling them in her arms she slid back into her own bed and fell asleep. When her parents found her in the morning light, she was still clutching the robe and the slipper. Wisely they said nothing about it and asked no questions. There is a delicacy which does not intrude upon the emotions of the vulnerable just because it is so vividly aware of them. For children it is one of the most precious of gifts and because of it they may share those very private, very personal emotions that live at the heart of individuality.

The right to privacy is the right to personal dignity. It is the right to open or close a door, to invite in a cherished friend or exclude the curious, the possessive, the arbitrary. The confidence which opens the door must be won. It cannot be commanded. That is as true for the young as for grown-ups. Wise parents wait for an invitation before approaching that door, and their children have no need for locks.

Love Is an Orange

WHEN I was a child, there was a good deal of adult conversation to the effect that children had to learn to be unselfish. It was a word that I came to dislike intensely because it always turned out to involve something I did not want to do and for the doing of which there were no discernible rewards. As I recall, the only benefit was a vague promise that "people" would like me whereas if I did what came naturally, there was grave doubt they would have any such tendency. Since the action desired by the grownups was always immediate and since it was never clear what good it was going to do me if in some vague distant future equally vague people did like me, the whole situation hardly seemed worth the trouble.

In my day what was specially stressed was showing unselfishness to other children which was in its effect adding insult to injury. You have a birthday party and invite all the little boys and girls you know to join the festivities. There is a fine, exciting flutter of activity, and you start counting up all the presents to be expected. You don't speak about this to the adults naturally because they would immediately pounce on this as another sample of selfishness. You're supposed to be all aglow with the thought of offering those perennial enemies next door a lovely dish of ice cream and cake. So you quietly total up the loot to be reasonably expected and indulge in a few foolish fantasies about whose parent just might crash through with that beautiful doll that sits neglected in a downtown window. You're conscious that this is wildly improbable, but you're young enough to believe that there could be guardian angels.

All this time the grownups blithely go ahead with a quite different set of ideas. They explain all the duties and obligations of a hostess, most of which are sure to spoil your fun. All of a sudden it seems you have to be polite to the very kids you've been fighting with right along. "Whose party is this anyway?" you say to yourself. If they had to be polite to you, that would be understandable. It's your birthday. Any reasonable child understands that there are certain occasions which entail certain prerogatives. What causes all the confusion is that adults turn everything topsy-turvy. They simply don't understand.

Anyway the great day comes. You're happy to note that under the watchful eye of grownups your guests are having to mind their manners too. Nevertheless the cards are stacked against you, a fact of which your charming little guests are also aware as you see from the gleam in their eyes. There is something about that gleam which warns you they're going to get even for what happened at their birthday parties. They do.

You dutifully start to pass the cake, ensconced in neat symmetrical squares on a company plate. Hastily you survey the pieces getting ready to extricate the biggest for yourself. At that moment some smiling grownup says sweetly, "Remember, you always serve your guests first, and you give the biggest pieces to them. You mustn't be selfish." You're licked, and you know it. You present the plate to your dear friends with the smallest pieces on their side in the dim hope they may have enough manners to pick the closest one. You're anything but surprised when they promptly reach across the whole plate to grab the biggest piece which was naturally on your side. Manners they don't have, and you knew it. Silently you promise them, "Wait until it's your birthday party." They say "Thank you" in loud sweet tones and silently beam their real answer "But I've got the biggest piece of cake *now*."

What really gets you, though, is that there is always some adult around to say brightly, "You see what nice manners your friends have. And how much nicer it is when you're unselfish." There are two dubious results of this kind of thing. One, you definitely lose a good bit of faith in adult intelligence and two, you get a considerably biased idea of unselfishness.

This is no argument against teaching manners to the young. On the contrary, it is a fine old tradition that ought to be resurrected from its current mothballs and put to work. Almost any child can learn that adults are entitled to a show of respect, that they are not to be interrupted in the middle of a sentence, treated as another kid, used as a convenient outlet for any and all impulses of the moment. In fact, children are much more comfortable when they know the guide rules for handling the social amenities. It's no more fun for a child to be introduced to a strange adult and have no idea what to say or do than it is for a grownup to go to a formal dinner and have no idea what fork to use. The idea that children feel free when allowed to run wild never originated with the children.

The trouble comes when adults want to teach children to

be polite to each other. This is the point where children and grownups part company. They simply don't operate on the same wavelengths. Children are willing, or can with a little persuasion become willing, to learn some of the necessary rules of the adult world, but grownups have practically no idea what the rules are in the child's world. In fact, they often don't know that there are rules. When in addition they want to "develop character" and "teach unselfishness" at the same time, the whole situation degenerates into a general confusion and a mass of subterfuge.

All children begin with the firm conviction that what they want or don't want is the most important consideration in the world and should be so regarded by all around them. This is natural enough because all they feel is concerned with themselves, and they've had no occasion to learn that other people also share this emotional lebensraum. To be honest most people to the end of their days feel their own headaches more vividly than those of the next guy.

Children learn shortly, however, that this free-wheeling assumption meets with a good many obstacles. Adults are not always their compliant handmaidens, and other children fight fiercely for that toy they just grabbed onto. This represents a very practical problem and has in a child's way of thinking absolutely nothing to do with any such confusing abstractions as character. If you reach for the gleaming new toy truck and another kid gets it first, the question is what you can do about it. You may not have the solution, but there is no confusion about the question. If an adult says to the other kid, "Now, Billy, let little David play with the truck. You're bigger than he is," that is for David a simple and effective solution to the problem and for Billy an unjust act of sabotage, backed by superior force and justified through the introduction of a totally irrelevant issue.

If the harassed adult wonders how one ever combines ethics with the grab-while-you-can rules of the young, the answer lies in a little judicious compromise. Billy got there first and by his lights is entitled to his victory. He also has to learn that in this world victory is rarely total or permanent. The intelligent grownup recognizes his ownership of the desired object but makes it clear that after a specified time it goes to David. He's entitled to his turn, and his size is neither advantage nor handicap. If neither party is likely to find this a totally satisfactory solution, neither will find it totally unsatisfactory either. That after all is the nature of compromise.

Life is full of such tricky and frustrating situations, and the dullest child learns that this is a perennial problem from which there is no escape. No matter what it is he wants there are usually others who want it too and hence don't want him to have it. Children, like adults, can get so caught up in this tug-of-war that what they're after becomes less important than preventing other people from getting it. A couple of two-year-olds will fight ferociously over the possession of a stuffed animal, and from their intensity an observer could only deduce that the animal is a highly prized possession. Five minutes later the winner can toss the prized possession into a corner with total indifference, and neither of the recent enemies will give it a second glance. The real cause of the battle was that ancient human need—I want what I want when I want it and I'm just the guy to see that I get it.

Obviously somebody has to lose out now and then, and the inevitable lesson comes home that everybody can't come first, and that practically nobody always does. This is a shock that people, however young, react to in various ways. Some never accept it at all and spend the rest of their lives insisting in one way or another that they are the victims of a hidden conspiracy. Some to the end of their days see it as a perpetual challenge to their powers of manipulation and whatever their defeats never lose sight of their original objective. Others grow up. The trouble with trying to teach children unselfishness by admonition is that it doesn't work. Like everyone else they have to learn from experience that "I come first" is not a recipe for life and somehow make their peace with the inevitable. When adults point some of the ways that peace can be made, growing up can be a lot smoother.

Children in time develop their own ground rules. These may bear the unmistakable stamp of expediency, but there is a certain wavering regard for the advantages of law and order. A friend of mine recently witnessed a fine example of legal judgment. A boy of eight or so was locked in bitter battle with a youngster two or three years younger over the possession of a large ball. Since the battle took place in the middle of a sidewalk, it began to attract attention. A young man of perhaps fifteen years approached the two contestants and broke up the fight. Gravely he inquired as to the cause of the fracas and was answered by a spate of heated remarks to the effect that each had prior right to said ball.

Upon investigation it turned out that neither had the original deed to the property. The ball had been left in the fruit store operated by the younger gentleman's father. When this boy took it out on the street for play, the older boy claimed it. The younger said this could not be correct because the older boy had not been in the fruit store, and further by the law of Finders Keepers the ball had clearly passed into the possession of the scion of the fruit store. There were two questions here. Was the older lying in order to take advantage of the ball's somewhat questionable ownership? Did the Finders-Keepers Law entitle the younger boy to ownership in any case? A further consideration was the possibility that the older boy might be seeking to exploit the youth and relative weakness of his young opponent.

The teen-ager considered all these questions, asked for further details and gravely gave each of the contestants an opportunity to defend his own case. He then rendered his verdict. The ball went to the younger boy because the Finders-Keepers Law was clearly on his side and because there was reasonable doubt that the older boy had ever been in possession of it. Both boys accepted his decision without further argument, and both seemed satisfied they had received a fair hearing. With that the judge proceeded on his way.

Neither boy had questioned his authority to arbitrate this dispute. While his superior size and age were clearly factors of importance here, the contestants had been most impressed by his judicial demeanor, his willingness to listen to both sides and his firm, unbiased confidence in his verdict. This was law and order with due process of respect for those most directly involved. It had nothing to do with such ambiguous abstractions as unselfishness, and it gave a feeling of security to the participants.

It is a pity that adults are so often too busy or too impatient to provide this kind of fair hearing to the disputes of the young. When children first ask for adult intervention, what almost invariably they desire is highly biased partisanship—in their own behalf of course. In effect they want to exploit the superior power of the grownup to compensate for their own

inability to make a successful grab. Parents have been known
to fall into this trap only to find themselves battling other
equally partisan parents in a ridiculous debate about who is
exploiting whom. At that point everybody operates on the "I
come first" line.

Aside from the pointless expenditure of energy this
leaves the young on the dead center of their own somewhat
primitive assumption that the biggest guy takes all. This is for
the wear and tear of daily living an uncomfortable assumption
as any intelligent child soon discovers. You never know when
someone bigger will happen along. A few steady rules can be
a great comfort well worth an occasional defeat. When a
grownup does take the time to listen to the flood of accusations and recriminations, sort out the embedded facts and provide a dash of elementary logic, he is likely to get a respectful
and even appreciative response from the participants, even if
the loser does indulge in a few frustrated tears.

The young appreciate also the compliment of serious adult
attention. No amount of partisanship, which after all operates
on the principle what's mine must be right, can hope to be so
reassuring and so solidly satisfying as the importance this
kind of attention attributes to the activities of the small people. Children are not slow to see that this sober, careful study
acknowledges their stature as persons of importance and
turns for winner and loser alike a tug-of-war into a dignified
procedure from which both sides emerge with a new victory.
They may even catch a first glimpse of the implications of
those mighty abstractions, law and order.

By and large the young are considerably more concerned
about being first with people than with things. They can battle briefly and furiously over a ball, but their real and continu-

ing concern remains with people. In the modern world this can often make them appear naive if not downright foolish. This concern does not arise of course from any humanitarian generosity. If you are dependent for survival upon a very few big people, those people are likely to be of considerable concern to you even discounting the fact that when they're good to you, you're apt to become very fond of them. Coming first with those vital few is in the nature of life insurance and not a paid-up policy either, life and chance being what they are.

It is all very well for the grownups to welcome a new arrival into a family. For the immediate predecessor it is no joke to have a new rival for the affections of those important few, particularly if he is still small. He's had enough struggle securing all the attention he wants without having to share what he has with someone still more helpless. There is good reason why the newcomer usually finds a ready ally in the big brother or sister two places beyond. That young man or woman observes accurately that the one who displaced him is now in turn being displaced. There is a classical satisfaction in welcoming the instrument of revenge and being praised by adults for one's nobility in doing so. It also contributes to the displaced one's sense of outrage and unjustified assault. After all he had nothing to do with the advent of the new intruder, and it is certain that he never regarded himself as occupying any similar position.

The considerable disparities in point of view among the various parties concerned account for the inordinate difficulties in what is known as preparing a child for the new baby. Parents have a natural tendency to emphasize how happy everyone is going to be, and since Johnny, age three, seems to display the most suspicion of this prospective felicity, they are apt to go a little overboard in describing the advantages to him personally. The resultant confusion can crescendo into the impasse that recently confronted friends of mine.

Being modern and enlightened they had carefully discussed with their three-year-old son the future arrival of a small brother or sister. He was interested and agreed that the whole situation should be a very pleasant one. His parents congratulated themselves on how smoothly the whole problem was being dissolved. If their small son displayed a certain lack of enthusiasm, this was, after all, only natural.

When the great day for mother's return from the hospital finally arrived, there was no question of the little boy's excitement. He had missed his mother and he had a full store of adventures waiting for her attentive ear. He was mildly annoyed when a strange infant arrived with her, but he was a polite little boy and was willing to wait a reasonable period of time for her full and undivided attention. In the meantime he agreed somewhat uneasily that the baby was very nice. It looked like any other baby to him, and the excitement of the adults was distinctly disquieting. Finally he had had enough and still polite inquired, "She's fine but when is she going home to her Mommy?" The rest seems best left to the imagination.

There probably is no fool-proof way of preparing any child for the fact that the most important people in his world have deliberately invited a small rival to share his hitherto peaceful existence and to infringe upon his exclusive prerogatives. When need is too great a part of love, there can be little room to share with others. Only the experience of love's stability that like a strong river flows on untouched by surface ruffles convinces anyone that a rival cannot steal but can join. The jealousy of the young is fear and a great need, and its solution is time and growth and experience.

An adolescent I once knew explained it very well. She had never had a real home, had lived with a series of foster families and therefore never belonged to anyone. She was extremely bright and although she would not have expressed it this way, she had a fair idea that she still had the needs of a small child. She once remarked, "When I love someone, I want all of that someone's attention. I don't want him to spend time or affection on anyone else." As she explained it, "To me love is like an orange. It has just so many sections. Every time the person I love gives a section to someone else, he takes it away from me. And I want the whole orange." With a smile she added, "I know with my brains that love is not really like that, that it is more like a balloon with an inexhaustible capacity. But my feelings say love is an orange." To the young, love is an orange.

Adults cannot give all the sections to the young even if they have them in the first place. But they might refrain from demanding a nobility that would stagger a saint. When mother boasts cheerfully, "Johnny is just crazy about his new little sister. He waits on her and watches her. You love her, don't you, dear?" Johnny hasn't much choice but to lie like a gentleman. Sometimes in the process he begins to lie to himself too, and then he begins to worry that something terrible may happen to little sister. She might get eaten by a stray tiger or fall into a tub of scalding water. There's usually a grownup around then, too, to remark, "Isn't that sweet? He worries about his little sister all the time." It doesn't often occur to that grownup to wonder why tigers and tubs of scalding water are all of a sudden wandering around the house waiting for an unwary moment.

There's no question that children's occasional homicidal impulses have to be banned. It simply isn't practical to let Johnny dump the baby on the floor. Little sister is there and he's got to learn to live with her. But neither should he have to pretend any sudden passion for her in order to preserve his own importance and place in the world. When all he has to do is tolerate her, he may discover with time and living that to his great surprise he misses her when she's not around. With enough time and enough living he may even learn that there is a balance of giving and getting and that with those we love giving may become getting.

↜15

Is Honesty
the Best Policy?

"WHY IS honesty the best policy?" The question, seriously asked, came from a troubled young adolescent. "What do people really mean by that?" she continued introducing further complication into what was already a tricky enough query.

My first impulse, like that of many adults, I suppose, was to respond with the proper moralistic lecture combined with a few well chosen examples of the pragmatic advantages of such morality as implied in that mundane little word "policy." On second thought the first question, let alone the second, did not appear so simple, and the standard answer with its vague, noble generalities might to an inquiring mind raise more questions than it answered. Various items from the daily newspaper nagged at my memory and made any answer to that second question a considerable hazard in the face of the ferocious logic of the young. Adolescents, particularly bright ones, have a frightening intolerance for so many of the comfortable evasions of the adult world.

The most expedient response was obviously to match question with question. "Why do you ask?" I inquired. "What happened?"

"Some of the kids in my Latin class cheat. When we have an exam they have translations hidden in their pockets, even up their sleeves."

"And you don't," I prompted.

She nodded. Then with a rush the gist of the problem appeared. "I study hard, learn the vocabulary, take my chances on the exam. But the kids who copy get just as good grades as I do and they don't spend half the time studying that I do."

I was relieved. This question wasn't going to be so difficult after all. "You may not get any better grades than they do," I pointed out, "but you will know Latin and they won't."

My young inquisitor shook her head unhappily. "The other kids say we'll never use Latin anyway so there's no need to know it. Once we're finished with the class, everyone will forget it anyhow." Uncomfortably I recalled my difficulty in understanding Latin phrases after four years of taking classes in it.

"Well," I said comfortingly switching my premise with celerity, "you will feel safe while you're taking the exam. You won't have to keep watching the teacher and worrying that at any moment she'll discover you are cheating."

"I don't think the kids worry about that," answered my remorseless Socrates sadly. "The teacher always stays at her desk. If she walked around the room, she'd see it easily enough, but she never walks around the room. I don't think she wants to find out and neither do the other kids. They say she doesn't want to make trouble any more than they do."

That rocked me back on my heels a bit. This wasn't turning out to be exactly simple. I was beginning to hunt for the advantages of that "best policy."

"Even if what you say is true, you still have the assurance inside yourself that you did the right thing. You can feel at peace with yourself. The other kids know it too and will respect your honesty."

"Oh no, they don't," answered my friend. "They tell me I'm a sucker for doing it the hard way when I'd be just as well off to copy and forget it. I'm doing all that work for nothing. They say if I was smart I'd stop being such a sucker. They're the ones who feel good. I just feel stupid, and I feel all mixed up. Maybe they're right. Maybe that is the most sensible thing to do."

I stared at her. There was no question that she was genuinely troubled. She didn't feel good. Finally I asked, "So why didn't you cheat? If there are no advantages to being honest in this situation, why didn't you copy like the others?"

"I don't know," she told me. "I don't see any reason not to, but I just couldn't do it. I feel as if there were something wrong with me that I couldn't. That's why I asked you. What do people mean that honesty is the best policy?"

What she had just described, of course, was conscience, that nagging, bewildering, remorseless, impractical high-water-mark of civilization. She had just had her first vivid lesson that it can be highly unpopular and that in this situation at least she'd be much more comfortable without it. Like all children and most adults she measured its efficacy against the immediate situation and judged its advantages and disadvantages accordingly. She was also in the process of experiencing the fact that even when the balance showed a debit, that turned out to be irrelevant. Her behavior might, in fact, be impractical, and

it certainly gave her no fine glow of satisfaction. She did not
even have the consolation of a firm conviction that she was
right. All she knew was what she could or could not do. Why
that was so, she did not know nor why some of her classmates
could take the easy short cut and others could not. Least of all
did she realize she was raising a crucial human question, perhaps the most crucial there is.

None of this is exactly easy to explain to a fifteen-year-old
girl who is understandably more concerned at the moment
with the immediate solution to her own problem than with
the fate of the world. Nevertheless she had raised the questions, and she was hunting for something that at least promised some clarification. Further, she was raising questions that
plague a good many people although she was only dimly
aware of this.

If what seemed right to her also seemed right to most of
the people around her, there would be no problem. As she
promptly observed, there would be no need to raise the question. Since this was not the case, her question was, "How do I
know which side is really right?" We turned that question
around. "Does popularity determine what is right and what is
wrong? If enough people do it, does that make it OK?" She
thought a lot of people did feel that way and with a wry smile
she admitted that sometimes she felt that way too. Also she
read the papers, and she knew that it was a point of view not
unknown among adults. It was certainly more comfortable
and it was a neat justification for taking the easy way to get
what you wanted and needed.

"What's wrong with taking the easy way?" she asked,
pinning me down as neatly as a lepidopterist mounting a butterfly. Sometimes there was nothing wrong, I conceded, or

else a lot of modern conveniences would be languishing in the moral shade. But what about the not infrequent circumstance when the easy way for one person meant a lot harder way for other people?

"So who got hurt in my Latin class?" she retorted.

"Maybe nobody," I admitted. "I wouldn't know. But what happens if some of the kids decide to cheat outside of the Latin class? You go to the store, and the butcher gives you second rate meat and charges you for first rate. You lend somebody money to help him out of a jam, and afterward he says he doesn't owe you anything because you didn't get his signature on a note that makes him legally responsible. Those are easy ways, too, to get what you want."

If everyone were like that it would be pretty awful my young friend considered. "Nobody could trust anybody else. You mean that if people cheat one place, they'll cheat other places too?"

I had to tell her that was not necessarily so. There are people who will cheat anywhere, anytime, given the chance, and although they rarely notice it, they end up most of the time cheating themselves worst of all. On the other hand, plenty of people will be honest in one kind of situation and cheat in another kind and still consider themselves honest and upright citizens. The truth is that only a very few persons are all of a piece without some bad flaws in the material somewhere. That doesn't make most people right, and it doesn't justify the flaws.

This thoughtful adolescent was struggling with some of the confusions and complexities of that continuing human struggle with conscience. Already she had tangled with some of the popular misconceptions, that it is natural, and hence to be taken for granted, particularly with people from "good families," that it confers a solid sense of righteousness, that it brings to its possessor some tangible rewards within a reasonable span of time. If all that were true, conscience would be much more common than it is and would be found in action, not in the glib phrases of regret or the soothing pretensions of language. Her behavior in the Latin class could easily be identified as conscience because even against her doubts, practical judgment, assurance of security from punishment she had to do what she did. In this one area of her life, at least, the time for debate and conflict and choice had passed, and conscience, jealous autocrat that it is, claimed first priority.

That young woman began life like everyone else with the firm conviction that what she wanted was justified by the fact she wanted it and no other considerations existed. Her first measuring stick was expediency. How in fifteen short years she could achieve the civilized compulsion of conscience, that is based after all on an abstract standard of behavior, is one of those quiet miracles of human growth and change that has yet to attract much human attention. Conscience is grown. Once rooted it may continue to grow for a lifetime or it may be warped and dwarfed before its first flowering. Like any living thing it requires the right climate, the right soil and continuing nourishment.

It is right here the adult world walks headlong into trouble. Grownups know the right words, and they can come easily. But children are not much interested in words. They persist with stubborn tenacity in watching what grownups do, and for better or for worse they by and large do likewise. A friend of mine used to say, "What a person is speaks so loudly a child cannot hear what he says." Nowhere is that more true than with conscience. For all those responsible for the lives of children—and that includes most people—this is no light matter. They didn't grow up with perfection either, and they carry their own battle scars. Children have a frightening capacity to make one feel naked, like those dreams of strolling into a crowded ballroom only to discover one hasn't so much as a pocket handkerchief to conceal one's nudity. They can strip away rationalizations, self-justifications, smooth-working self-deceptions in one devastating, imitative action with an unawareness of the damage that is even more frightening. They did what the adults did, and it must be all right because the adult did it first. It is like living with one of those magic mirrors from the fairy tales.

The growth of conscience is much more than imitation. It is symbolic cannibalism. The savage ate the heart of a brave man to gain his courage. One could observe that this was an attempt to acquire virtue the instant way. How successful it was is not clear. For the child of civilization it is more difficult. The values and standards of those adults closest to him must not only be absorbed but woven into the whole fabric of his personality until he is no longer aware of their separate existence. He cannot absorb what those adults say—although he can imitate it—but only what they are. For this only the ruthless honesty of reality can serve. The faults as well as the virtues of the important grownups are ingested and digested to become part of the life pattern of the future. The self-deceptions as well as the self-truths become part of that remorseless process.

This is much more than the acquisition of customs and manners, the schooling in what is and is not proper and acceptable. That is important but it remains always on the sur-

face of personality like the scaffolding on a building. Conscience or the lack of it lives at the heart of a person and per-
vades who and what he is. It determines what he will or will
not do when the chips are down. Conscience commands from
within and when it is strong and clear it has no concern with
what is popular or expedient or even, at its most powerful,
with the price tag attached.

When the Nazis overran Yugoslavia, they searched with
methodical deadliness for the chief Rabbi. Fleeing from certain
death he sat in a railroad station of a small town waiting for
the one train that might carry him to safety. A scarf wrapped
about his throat half hid the beard that could identify him, the
beard he was too proud to abandon. A man walking by
stopped suddenly, his eyes widening with recognition. Without a sound he continued walking, patrolling the station platform. A little later he returned and said softly to the Rabbi,
"Come with me." He lead the way to a small empty room and
whispered, "Stay here until I come for you." A moment later
the train platform filled with a group of German soldiers, and
a Nazi officer yelled commands. When finally the train arrived, there was a confusion of sound and movement with
people pushing back and forth. The soldiers checked on all
those getting into the train. Moments passed and the train
blew a warning whistle for departure. Only then did the
stranger return to the small room and again said to the Rabbi,
"Follow me." Deftly he lead the way to a rear car already
checked by the Nazi guards. As the Rabbi climbed aboard,
the train began to move. The stranger slid back into the crowd.

The Nazis never found the chief Rabbi. The man who
saved his life recognized him but did not know him. The
stranger was a Serb, not Jewish, and in a conquered land he

could have gained valuable privileges for himself by inform-
ing the Germans. He had only death to expect if he were discovered aiding the escape of a wanted man, above all this man.
Why did he risk his life and perhaps that of his family for a
man he did not know, a man who was never even to know his
name? The answer is conscience. He did it for himself. In the
midst of madness the clear, quiet voice of sanity spoke, and
because of it a man lived.

Conscience at its full maturity is not concerned with guilt
and remorse and self-punishment. It is the heart of identity,
and it can be violated only at the cost of irreparable damage
to the whole personality. Only the very few ever achieve a
conscience grown to full maturity. The way is too long and
too hard.

The child begins with the first wobbling steps of necessity. He learns to do or not to do certain things against the
imperiousness of his own wishes either because he wishes to
please a mother and father he loves or because he fears their
disapproval and punishment. He does not see anything wrong
in what he wishes, but he learns to have an eye for their
consequences. His concern is not for the action but for its discovery. There are those who never grow beyond this step.
All their life they are checked only by the fear of discovery
and punishment. Perhaps as children they were actuated more
by fear than by the wish to please. Had one of them strolled
that station platform in Yugoslavia, the Rabbi would have
died.

With time, a child begins to absorb into himself the atti-
tudes and feelings and qualities of those closest to him. Then
for the first time he begins to feel a little of the power of conscience. Even when a disapproved action is not discovered, he

feels uncomfortable and anxious. Something seems to be wrong although he does not know what. Sometimes he betrays the very action that had been so successfully concealed and wonders at his own foolishness and even feels relieved. For the first time the action itself troubles him, and although he does not yet understand it, he is feeling the intimations of his own disapproval. The disapproval of a mother and father is becoming his, and while he can hide from them, he cannot lose himself. As yet conscience is no integral part of his being. It is more like a nagging mosquito that he cannot escape. There are people who stop at this step. They continue to do or not to do things of which they disapprove and afterward battle themselves and others to escape the discomfort.

The fortunate children who learn integrity at home may move slowly to take the big step, to give power to conscience, to make the standard of right itself a part of their pattern of life. The nature of that standard will depend upon their teachers, but once it has become a part of them, it will be theirs whether their teachers are there or not. It can have its weaknesses, it can falter because strength does not grow at a bound, but it will endure.

The nature of that standard and the way it was taught will have great effect not only upon the life of the individual, but upon the lives of those who will be important to him. If he learned chiefly through fear, fear will live with him and inflict others as well as himself. If he learned chiefly through love, love will live with him and illumine the lives of others as well as his own. He will pass on what was passed on to him. For most people that is a mixture of strength and weakness, sureness and confusion, conscience and lack of conscience. Yet one side does predominate. There are those who despite doubt and wavering and confusion do listen and obey the inner command of conscience. And there are those who despite brave words require the policeman to command what they cannot require of themselves.

Is honesty the best policy? Perhaps the answer depends on the length and breadth of the judgment. Is conscience worth its great cost and ceaseless struggle? There are those who would surely say no because they do not even notice that their very survival is possible only because others have said yes. Without conscience civilization is impossible because no laws and no force can substitute for the self-enforced standards that extend their power to all those in need of it. It is not in its immediate, material benefit to the individual that conscience displays its grandeur, but in its power to lift human beings to the height of their aspirations. To grab what one wants like a two-year-old is easy and belongs with the primitivity of man's long infancy. To live by the conscience of maturity is incredibly difficult and is the hope of civilization.

When the world knows the stranger on the station platform as the greatest of its heroes, humanity will finally come of age.

Watch Your Stomach

ONE HARDLY has time to draw the first full breath upon admission to this peculiar planet before encountering its "do's" and "don'ts." There is no escaping them before the last breath of existence has fluttered into silence. Rules, authority, punishment beset the bewildered and rebellious young, and their elders continue the struggle. Without them there can be no order, and they are the harbingers of that long, difficult evolution we call conscience.

Almost no one seems to become totally reconciled to them, and a considerable number of people never make up their minds what they intend or don't intend to do about them.

There are those who approve of some of them and want to throw the rest in the ashcan. There are those who like practically none of them and dream of a peaceful anarchy. Then there are the ones who approve in principle but think the current batch is all wrong and want to substitute their own variety. Some people regard them as a challenge to their ingenuity in the development of evasive techniques, if not an incitement to contradiction, while others invest them with an aura of divine revelation and the majesty of universal fiat. For children they are a labyrinth full of concealed hazards and unexpected trials and once in a while a stretch of cleared path refreshingly sunlit. None of this turns out to be precisely simple despite the interminable centuries humans have been tinkering with the whole problem.

My two-year-old niece neatly bit me on the arm one day for no reason that was immediately obvious to me. In outraged tone I said, "Don't do that." She stared at me with that unwinking blankness possible only to psychotics and the very young. Still outraged I asked, "Why?"

"Because I wanted to," was her lucid response.

With adult illogic I retorted, "Well, stop wanting to."

She considered that in silence and then volunteered, "I'm a mosquito."

"Well, stop being a mosquito," I ordered.

The point, of course, is that no coherent system of prohibitions is likely to cover the hazards of a two-year-old girl who turns into a mosquito. It is not the kind of thing that spontaneously occurs to most adults. Yet with small children it is only one more example of the exigencies that can and do arise on any ordinary day. It has driven grownups into all kinds of systems and theories, more or less foolish, that promise to turn the young into the well-behaved little models of virtue that happen to be approved at any given moment in history. These theories and systems have made for some astonishing contradictions.

There is the rather hoary one that made adult authority into a good firm strait-jacket with a lifetime guarantee. According to that point of view, a question was just about as bad as a violation, and neither was to be tolerated. Adults were adults, and children were children. One commanded, and the

other obeyed. It had a nice ring of simplicity, but there is some
question that it was an unadulterated success. It precluded a
good bit of what in modern jargon is known as communication. Even under that heavy-handed approach there must
have been adults who let a few questions and violations slip
through when the neighbors weren't looking.

In recent years there has been a new theory. According to
this one grownups just sit back and endure while the young
stumble around and find the right paths by trial and error. It's
supposed to develop initiative, and if adults survive, an ultimate accessibility to the uses of reason that should solve a
good many problems. There are variations on this one too,
and quite a few do's and don'ts slip in to becloud the issue. To
add to the general confusion the nature of the do's and don'ts
keeps shifting, and some parents feel the whole matter should
be left up to the school anyway. What's teacher training for?

Naturally, the children regard the whole problem from a
totally different point of view. As pragmatists they're less interested in the theory than in what works for them. That is
usually different from what works for grownups. As devotees
of the immediate result they have almost no interest in future
developments or ultimate benefits. As realists they never lose
sight of the fact and uses of power. Any child with normal
interest in self-preservation makes it a first order of business in
any situation to identify the chief source of authority. In
other words, who is the boss?

Going through channels is, in the estimation of most children, a bore, not to mention a waste of perfectly good time
and effort. They prefer to go straight to the top until they
learn, of course, that intermediaries have their uses and can
sometimes be subverted to sympathetic ends. They are uncan-

nily astute in perceiving who wields the real power in any situation and never confuse, the official with the actual. They have a direct and rather simple view of power. It is also a highly practical one.

Their first question is whose orders are obeyed. Who sees to it that things do or do not happen. Their second concern is where is the geographical whereabouts of that person. If he's frequently at some distance, then his power is not something to be counted on. It may work fine when he's present, but what happens when he's gone. To children, visibility and power are just naturally twins, and the idea of an authority strong enough to be reckoned with that is not personally and visually present or at least within yelling distance leaves them cold. That's why the firmest prohibitions have a tendency to dissolve when their enforcers are absent for any considerable period.

When one is small, it is also hard common sense. The babysitter who is big enough and mean enough to twist one's arm has the power that counts when parents are gone. Even the threat to tell on her may not be very potent because, as every child knows, adults can't be depended on to listen too carefully to what a child says, especially if he's still pretty small.

Adults have a much more complicated view of power. They are aware that there are several different kinds, and they invest them with various moral and material values. There is the power of influence that can get you what you want or upon occasion inflict upon you what you don't want. There is the power of an abstract force like government that can become alarmingly concrete under certain circumstances. There is the power of custom, of what other people expect of you, not so much specific individuals as that amorphous "they." There is the power of physical force and the power of moral conviction. One way or another adults are concerned with power all their days, but children practically never believe this.

They take it for granted that grownups are omnipotent if not omniscient. When you are big, you can do as you please. There are no rules you cannot break with impunity, and there's no one to tell you you can't go out in the snow or have a second dish of ice cream. One of the most frequent and plaintive of admonitions upon the lips of the small is, "You could if you wanted to." It's a delightful fantasy and adults wish it were true. They have learned what cannot be explained—that there is a future as well as a present and that invisible power may be very potent.

The real trouble is that they get pretty mixed up about what they think about all this. They approve law and order, but they respond with a thrill of pleasure to a spot of anarchy now and then. They recognize the beneficial results of traffic lights, but they do get a secret delight in sneaking through a red one, happily unobserved by the representatives of the law. They believe in paying their bills and maintaining a solid credit rating, but it can brighten a whole day to have the telephone send back their dime with a bright bonus of nickels. The real pleasure in life's small rebellions is getting away with them. After that you can boast about them and spice up the details while you watch the faint cloud of envy in the eyes of your friends. There is, in fact, within the heart of the average solid citizen a well-defined contempt for the grownup who never thumbs his nose at the powers that be once in a while without getting caught.

This can be quite confusing to children who feel this way about practically all do's and don'ts. For them the major problem is that most of these commands that hedge them in from morning to night simply don't make sense in terms intelligible to them. They enjoy getting away with a little larceny as well as the next man, but they don't understand why it has to stop at a little nor why grownups grin at one kind and are horrified or furious at another. Just to complicate the situation further, not all adults grin or get furious at the same things, and there's nothing for it but to learn from experience which grownup is likely to do what. Every child of course concentrates on those grownups that carry the power over them at any given time, but even this is difficult enough.

One little girl with a lively sense of her own dignity was called an insulting name by another little girl who shared the first grade with her. Outraged the young lady promptly hit her persecutor in the mouth, a good solid blow that knocked out a tooth that was about to fall out anyway. The teacher was horrified. Proper little girls don't knock the teeth out of other little girls' mouths even when they do say unpleasant words. The small pugilist's mother was also horrified, particularly since both the teacher and the victim's parents had called with vociferous complaints.

Everyone was saying that small girls did not do this kind of thing which seemed to leave the small girl in question in a state of chilly isolation. Then along came her father and he said it too, only with a certain reservation in his tone that seemed to denote something less than wholehearted consternation. The small girl, who by this time had been practically convinced of her moral degeneracy, took a long look at him and with unerring judgment glued herself to his side. That evening when no one was close he whispered hastily, "Little girls really shouldn't go around knocking people's teeth out. All the same I'm proud of you." Papa had a point there but there's no use pretending that he clarified the issue.

Adults are forever bewailing in such situations. "What can you do?" A little common sense to the effect that words can be just as much an act of aggression as blows would certainly have helped. Also, one punch doesn't make an Amazon nor one insult obliterate even a first-grader. That is naturally common sense for adults, not first-graders, who considered the solution to the whole fracas a simple matter of adults using their authority to confirm that each was absolutely right. If grownups were foolish enough to divide along kinship lines, let alone philosophical abstractions, that is clearly no concern of children.

This is just what upsets adults. They are not only required to analyze the situation with some degree of objectivity but to exercise authority with the conviction that springs from the sure knowledge that the way is clear. Children are alert always for the hint of doubt in a look, an expression, a tone of voice. Like a termite chewing away at the rafters, doubt is definitely subversive to the full expression of authority. Children both welcome and fear it. It's a fine entering wedge for widening the gaps in do's and don'ts that have to be respected. It also leaves children with the uneasy feeling that a wall that should be strong enough to withstand any battering might suddenly give way, tumbling them into helpless panic.

It leads adults into substituting noise for conviction. If they're not sure they are right they can always try to get the same effect by yelling. Since children rapidly become impervious to any amount of noise, this rarely leads to anything but more confusion. The trouble is, doubt is a more or less chronic state in today's world. The old verities have lost a good bit of their punch, and some of them have plainly gone into discard. Who knows when conviction may turn out to be nothing more than dogma or principles earn only the appellation of old-fashioned. It is perhaps comprehensible that some adults settle for a rule-of-thumb that what gets on their nerves is wrong and for the rest children should stay out of trouble with the neighbors and the authorities.

The only other solution involves adults in examining their own beliefs and finding their own way through to convictions that they can live by regardless of what the neighbors think. This is authority children respect even when they disagree with it, and it has the consistency that is a great help in finding one's way through the intricacies of everyday life. It has the strength that children can lean on with no fear of collapse. It also has a high price tag for grownups who have to find their own way in situations their great grandparents never dreamed of with little of the comforting consensus those esteemed ancestors took for granted.

Adults, in fact, also suffer from lack of authority, and like the children, they have a decidedly mixed reaction to that fact. Both grownups and children like to know where they stand and what is expected of them, and they prefer continuity in those matters. They have their moments of rebellion, and they like to take a swipe at the rules now and then to show they've got some spirit. But what fun is a little light-hearted rebellion if the rules collapse at the first spirited tap? What happens to the prodigal son when he returns home to find that the whole family has gone prodigal? It's a lot more unsettling to have to build your own rules than to indulge in some youthful defiance of those already in efficient operation.

Children can't make their own rules and no child is happy without them. The great need of the young is for authority that protects them against the consequences of their own primitive passions and their lack of experience, that provides them with guides for everyday behavior and that builds some solid ground they can stand on for the future. It is no help to Johnny to be allowed to hit baby brother over the head with a solid wooden block, and it is certainly no help to baby brother. Johnny feels like hitting so he hits but he has no knowledge of, and less concern for, future consequences, and futhermore this is no recipe for a peaceful life. He has to be stopped until he has the strength and conviction to stop himself. It is no kindness to let him walk into deep water when he can't swim and doesn't know that deep water is dangerous to him. It is no fun for him to have no idea of what to do when he eats with grownups, goes into the houses of parental friends, meets new adults. Like anybody else he requires education, and at the beginning education grows in the framework of authority.

A friend of mine was walking in the park with an unhappy little boy who sustained himself by fighting all rules with a fine impartiality. If someone said "Yes," he said "No," and never noticed that his every move was by this method dictated by someone else. On this day they came to a sign "don't pick the flowers," and like an old fire horse the boy headed for the flower bed. My friend put her arm around him and said firmly, "No, you'll get into trouble doing that. I'm not going to have you getting into trouble, not when I'm here to prevent it." In astonishment the youngster walked by the flower bed. There was nothing to fight.

This is authority that protects the young. It is not the kind that people battle and resent. Children can get mad for the moment but that doesn't weigh very heavily against the security of protection. It is rather sad that the word authority more often than not brings to people an association of something unpleasant, something to be escaped or outgrown. "When I'm big I'll do as I please," says the small one. When he's big, the only thing that has changed is the nature of the rules. The only real escape is to grow the ability to provide and enforce one's own authority over one's own life. That is very hard work and not at all childlike.

There can be few phenomena more confusing in an admittedly confusing world than the uncertainty many parents feel about their right to say yes or no to their children. There is a feeling abroad that parents don't know how to make decisions for their children anymore, and that because man can get to the moon, two everyday grownups can't possibly figure out how to guide their youngsters according to some basic time-tested values into leading a useful and sensible life. By some technological miracle the children are supposed to find that out for themselves. There is no intrinsic conflict between electronics and the development of solid character in human beings unless of course people decide that only the former is important. Grownups are still in a better position than children to know something about the complexities and realities of life even if as adults those children will someday travel faster and farther than their parents ever did.

No one knows better than children how much they need the authority that protects, that sets the outer limits of behavior with known and prescribed consequences. As one little boy expressed it to his mother, "You care what I do." I heard two young girls just coming into adolescence saying much the same thing. One said proudly, "My mother has a fit if I'm out after eleven o'clock. She wants to know who I go out with, where I go, and she won't let me stay out late." The other girl said sadly, "My mother doesn't care what I do." Children can get mad at limits. But what kind of a world is this if children can't get mad at their own parents without adults running up a flag of surrender?

Children have a lively sense, too, of the legitimacy of authority. Any big sister who ever tried to boss the little ones knows that monotonous and to big sister infuriating response, "You're not my mother, I don't have to do what you say." They usually don't, either. Certain people are entitled by the nature of their position to be boss, and anyone else is obviously a usurper. Once in a while a member of the young is willing to give consideration to another possible rationale for the privilege of ordering him around. I remember one young friend of four who was engaged in some nefarious activity from which I forcibly removed him. I placed him firmly in a chair and returned to the fascinating job of washing dishes.

He regarded me with resentment and finally remarked, "You can't make me stay here with you. You're not my mother. I don't have to do what you say."

"That's true," I agreed, "but I think you will do what I said."

"Why do you think so?" he inquired with a spark of interest.

"Because you like me and I like you," I answered with sincerity if not precise relevance.

He considered that one in silence for a long moment and then apparently decided it was valid. "Did you see what happened to Peanuts in the paper tonight?" he inquired cheerfully. The conversation settled down into sociable lines.

I suppose nothing has given authority such a bad name as its constant association with punishment. People are forever asking, "What is the right way to punish a child?" They worry whether a spanking will harm the psyche of the young while prohibition on desserts might correct it. Or would it? Those who proudly refer to themselves as "old-fashioned" —by which they mean they're the only ones with common sense—prefer some form of physical violence while others take the psychological route and get themselves tangled in abstruse possibilities. Neither of them talk much about the kind and purpose of the authority which presumably developed a fracture since punishment is normally considered only after an infraction of the rules that be. The situation is roughly comparable to everybody arguing what fine should be exacted from two drivers who met at an intersection without ever considering whether a traffic light might be the solution.

Every child needs to be stopped at innumerable intersections, and sometimes punishment is the only way he learns the matter is serious enough to occupy his attention for any span of time. Mostly this is not much of a problem or would not be except for grownups who get so involved in their own pressures, confusions and irritations that they can't see the wood for the trees. When harassed adults are not harassed, they think about the purpose of authority and how to achieve that purpose. In one small town two junior citizens of approximately four years watched fascinatedly the painting of the neighbor's garage. They chatted happily with the painters who were friendly souls, and they admired the gleaming white result. There stirred in their hearts a wish to express their own artistic impulses on so prominent a canvas. The re-

sult was an interesting abstract design in green splashing gaily
to the height of a four-year-old's reach.

The neighbors, being of the conventional type, didn't care
too much for the design. The parents of the artists were involved in such non-artistic concerns as trespassing on other
people's property and making financial restitution, matters
which had certainly not occurred to the artists in question.
Yet the grownups were more amused than perturbed. Therefore their deliberations were rational and realistic in the best
tradition of maturity. While the parents paid for the damage,
they sent the budding artists to the neighbors to make their
peace and work out some of the financial complications on
their own. It was finally agreed that a nickel a week should be
abstracted from their respective allowances until the sum of
one dollar each had been paid. The children were impressed
by their own financial competence and the solemnity of the
procedure. While a nickel is a nickel and no young artist can
afford to be blithe about it, it is dubious that these two felt
punished. They acknowledged the justice of the verdict, and
they felt a new importance for this grown-up concern, responsibility.

The true question is not "what kind of punishment" but
"what kind of authority." Children want the kind that
serves their needs and adults too often indulge in the kind that
serves their own. This is, of course, an inevitable consequence,
at least to some extent, so long as the adult population is made
up of human beings. To turn grownups into candidates for
sainthood would be nice but is probably not very practical.
On the other hand there is no clear reason why big people
shouldn't make use of intelligence and rationality to strike a
medium, even if it isn't always a happy one.

Priority can be given to do's and don'ts deemed essential, and it is possible to come up with some pretty solid essentials. Hitting baby brother over the head with a baseball bat doesn't need to be equated with stepping in a mud puddle. There is a clearly practical difference in consequence. Even if stepping in a mud puddle does grate on grown-up nerves upon occasion, there can be some small leeway between youthful exuberance and adult irritability. Grownups might even become sufficiently thoughtful to expect a few such catastrophes and provide themselves with an occasional escape valve. That might even be a help in promoting some valuable consistency. The best way to reduce authority to the level of eccentricity is to forget all about continuity and leave the command to the mood of the moment. That drives any sane child wild even when he learns how to turn it to his own fleeting advantage. At its best authority is an orderly instruction in life with self-discipline its goal and responsibility its substitute for blame.

Grownups often declaim, "How do you discipline children?" Discipline is a growth not a discovery. It is not its ups and downs that matter but its direction. There are only two reasons why any child decides to give up something he wants to do or to do something he doesn't like. One is fear, and punishment is the enforcer. The other is the wish to please someone important, and love is the enforcer. Normally in everyday life both find their place and necessarily so. The important question is which predominates and grows into the prime determiner of behavior. When it is fear, the outside rules and the power of their enforcement tell the story. When it is love, self-discipline builds the structure of conscience. The child who has no authority upon which to depend is like a leaf in the wind, and too often he is a menace to himself and to those about him.

For grownups, perhaps the best advice was inadvertently given by one of the young. He was discussing the subject from a rather peripheral viewpoint. He was disgusted at the moment with the women in his life and was announcing in loud tones what he was prepared to do "to show the women."

With malice aforethought I inquired, "Are you sure it's the women you want to show?"

He stopped short and glared at me suspiciously. "Now what have you got on your mind?" he demanded belligerently.

"I just wondered if it was really the women you are so anxious to show," I repeated.

"I suppose you mean it's really myself I want to show," he answered sullenly. Imgaine grownups letting themselves in for that!

"God gave you a good mind. Use it," was my weasely response.

He thought that one over and then inquired sweetly, "Where is my mind?"

After considerable discussion that would have horrified a professional philosopher, we settled on the fact that what people mean by mind can be the brain in your head or the combination of sense and feeling that some say resides in the heart and others insist belongs in the stomach. "The Chinese think it is the stomach," I added learnedly.

"I agree with the Chinese," my young friend advised promptly.

He's probably right. The best advice for any adult may be—watch your stomach.

◆ 17

The Caterpillar
That Never Became
a Butterfly

FOR CENTURIES philosophers have argued and debated. Is man born bad, the evil deep in his bones and guts to be somehow tamed and kneaded and worked into acceptable shape? Or is he born good, innocent of any knowledge of evil until the world's corruption infects him, too, with its fatal virus? These days we incline to the latter view although we act sometimes as though the former were our true belief.

We look at the baby and see his helplessness and confuse that with virtue. We see the innocence of his fresh young face and forget that innocence may be little more than lack of experience. Evil he is not. Yet does that make him good? Like Adam and Eve in the Garden of Eden he has yet to taste of the tree of knowledge and to know that either good or evil exist. In the meantime he is quite simply himself, concerned with his own affairs and happily unaware of the complicated demands and debates of his elders. Yet he is not a small, clean slate upon which those elders may write whatever message they wish. He brings his own desires and seeks his own means to their answer. With all the force of his own small person he flings himself against those unceasing demands which are so strangely labeled good and bad.

It is good to be quiet and bad to cry. It is good to laugh at the small clatter of the spoon dropped from the high chair tray and bad to keep dropping it for grownups to rescue. It is good to smile at the guest in the house and bad to nip his finger when he pokes it in a soft cheek. It is good to cuddle the squishy teddy bear and bad to hurl it at the head of an irritating grownup. It is good to admire the gay parade of yellow ducks on a white china mug of milk and bad to fling it at the floor and enjoy the fine satisfaction of its crash. It is good to listen to the tick of the clock with ardent fascination and bad, very bad, to go looking for the source of that interesting sound. Grownups say, "Children are so destructive. I'll be glad when they learn to take care of things like us." It's interesting how they always specify "things."

Children are destructive. Sometimes they are anxious and want to know what is inside. Sometimes they like to hear the crash and tinkle of falling things, as soothing as a waterfall. Sometimes they are angry and find in the hurled weapon a useful supplement for feeble strength or try a good solid bite with jaws more effective than hands. Sometimes they like to demolish just for the sheer exuberance of destruction. The small one builds his tower of blocks with loving care and thoughtful concentration and then with one merry sweep of his arm he sends them tumbling in noisy chaos. He laughs with delight as he demolishes with a gesture what he has built with the small intricacies of creation. It is the impulse that can make even the lordly adult uneasy in a china shop.

In every child there is the joy of creation and the joy of destruction. Which grows at the expense of the other depends upon which nurturing climate grownups provide for their young. Life keeps its own books and adds its own totals, and no man may juggle those inexorable figures. For better or worse the direction is set, to create much and destroy little, to create some and destroy some, to create little and destroy much. There are those who turn destruction upon themselves and those who turn its fury upon the world around them, and both destroy. For those who create, they and the world become partners in benefit.

It is strange in a world threatened with destruction by man's own hand that grownups see the destructiveness of children as a nuisance and a phase, a little like cutting teeth, that will pass with time and a modicum of endurance. It is a phase that threatens to outlast us all. The strength of the young is feeble and their weapons puny, but the violence of their wish, now flickering and transient, holds the seeds of power and permanence. With anger, fear, hatred and deprivation that wish to destroy may grow into a giant. With love and safety, fulfillment and laughter, it flickers and weakens and seeks for ways to transform itself into that which serves life.

Nothing about the human young is more wonderful, more awesome, than their ability to change iron into gold, to transform the destructive into the creative, to substitute for the near-sighted directness of the primitive the complex simplicity of the civilized. It takes them a little time and quite a bit of grown-up help, but the true miracles always take time and are so quiet that only the perceptive observe their emergence.

I remember a little boy who like many another member of the young had discovered that throwing stones could be an exciting sport. If he was mad at his mother, he could always go outside and throw stones just close enough to a passer-by to create consternation in the innocent wayfarer and a fine glow of satisfaction in himself. It was already substitution of a sort but not much transformation. Both his mother and the passer-by were inclined to regard the activity as nefarious and to take remarkably little interest in his glow of achievement. The vigorous remonstrances of his parents were regarded by him as inevitable, subduing but less than completely efficacious.

Then his parents had an inspiration. They set up a stone-throwing range with a sound wooden board for target. Sensibly isolated it offered no opportunity for damage and mayhem. Here, they told him, he could throw stones to his heart's content, but everywhere off range stones were for looking only. There's no use pretending the young David found a shabby board as satisfying as a casual Goliath, but it was something. Reluctantly he trimmed his activities to the wind of necessity. Imagination and fantasy were some help, and fortunately no one inquired into their substance. In time of course he got tired of throwing stones at symbols but then he discovered balls and games. That began to be something quite different again.

The little boy can continue to get mad at all kinds of people, but so long as he doesn't have to get mad too long, too often, too much he is on his way to enjoying a new game. That opens up totally new possibilities and in fact is quite a different matter. He may, of course, end up as just another spectator at the World Series, but by then aggression may have shrunk to the time-honored yell of "Kill the umpire."

One day I was walking with a three-year-old friend of mine and we came across a fat, fuzzy caterpillar crawling laboriously across the sidewalk. He was instantly interested in this odd creature and stopped to examine it. He was about to terminate the encounter and incidentally the caterpillar by stepping on it when I intervened.

I told him the whole story of how the caterpillar spun a cocoon, retired from active life and emerged a beautiful, graceful butterfly. My friend listened with that flattering concentration which is so soothing to the adult ego. When I finished the story, I was convinced it had made a deep impression on my small friend. Maybe it had but not precisely the kind I had in mind. I turned away to resume our walk, and he said, "Just a minute." He went back and stepped on the caterpillar and then said cheerfully, "Let's go." With luck a couple of years later he will settle for poking a stick in front of another fat, fuzzy caterpillar and laugh at its earnest attemps to circumvent the obstacle. The caterpillar may take a dim view of this too, but it will live to become a butterfly and warn its grandchildren. With still more luck and another ten years or so my small friend will lift the caterpillar out of harm's way and enjoy the butterfly.

The luck he needs is grownups who have tamed their own destructiveness, who can look at a caterpillar without an uncontrollable yen to step on it. Most important of all they are not destructive to him. That doesn't mean they can't say "No" to him or punish him upon occasion. Quite simply they don't use him as a convenient vent for their own unhappy feelings, a scapegoat for the actions they dare not turn upon their true objectives. A child has small means to gain control of his own violence when it is incited by those against whom he dare not retaliate. He learns what he has been taught—to turn destruction upon a living creature that cannot hit back. He becomes the bully and the weakling who thinks himself a conqueror because he steps upon a caterpillar. My small friend was still happily free of any such delusions. He stepped on the caterpillar because he felt like it, and he didn't think himself anything. At his age his private world was a closed circle that encompassed the universe. Nothing truly existed outside it. He liked the story of the caterpillar and the butterfly, but that had nothing to do with stepping on a fuzzy worm crawling across the sidewalk.

He had the destructiveness of the very young who are oblivious of any pain but their own. As consciousness widens the world, there comes a break in the closed circle. The young learn that the world is full of people and creatures who also feel and know pain. Then they must turn one way or the other, toward destroying or protecting, and this time with awareness that they destroy or protect. With luck they have grownups who protect them and they begin the difficult, wonderful process of becoming civilized.

One of the most powerful nudgers in that process is humor, perhaps because in its true essence it is always the enemy of destructiveness. Children place a high value on it. Intuitively they know it is their ally. They never mistake the cruelty of the practical joke or the sting of mockery for the light-footed clarity of humor. They know that in the presence of laughter adults forget their irritations, lose their fierceness and become more gentle, even more reasonable, and everyone feels good. They can laugh at all kinds of small things because they are still new enough to see that the world is full of comical sights and sounds. The antics of a kitten with a string, the sound of a new word, the tickle of a feather and the spontaneity of their delight can bring freshness to the jaded eyes of their elders.

Their own sense of humor is not particularly subtle. They love slapstick. They thoroughly enjoyed open-toe shoes because there was a whole vista of opportunity for tickling nylon-clad toes unexpectedly. The unexpected part is important because nothing amuses the young like catching their elders offguard. They like to hide behind convenient chairs and come bursting out like a jack-in-the-box to yell "Boo." There is, of course, a streak of cruelty in slapstick, but that is exactly why it is so useful to small people. They can gain a momentary advantage over the big people, enjoy a flash of power, but it is all a game that everyone can enjoy. The fangs are pulled, and the wish to hurt has been reduced to the dimensions of a joke. A rock in the face is vicious, but a pie in the face is funny.

Generations of children have laughed at the clown who is forever stumbling into pails of water, falling over his own feet, getting hit with boards and never getting hurt. The children know it is a game, that it is all pretend and they are free to enjoy it. The pie has substituted for the rock and laughter for destruction. A little girl I knew devoted a happy hour to the game of almost biting my finger. At the moment of danger I hastily withdrew it from range of her sharp little teeth which clicked together with ominous portent. She enjoyed this with wholehearted pleasure because the game translated the undoubted wish to bite somebody—a wish the human young are almost universally heir to—into a suspense drama with a slapstick ending. Humor has taken a gigantic first step and with the magic of laughter has changed the destructive into the innocuous.

A game is not the same as humor, but for children they are first cousins. A game may walk through shadows but its destination is the open sunlight. It has that mixture of reality and illusion that opens avenues of escape to the hard-pressed young with the boon of impunity. "Let's play house," say the young ones, and adults can be caricatured with ruthless accuracy. Adults practically never watch anyway and are happy to settle for the casual indifference of, "The children are only playing." Grownups have their own games to absorb their attention.

My eight-year-old nephew, with a band of friends, spent a peaceful summer morning fighting a war from behind the walls of a homemade fort of Revolutionary War vintage. I have no knowledge of the outcome of the battle, but around noon my nephew dashed in with that common human complaint, an empty stomach. I agreed to supply the army with sandwiches and lemonade, and he had begun his dash back to the safety of the fort. Suddenly he reversed himself. "I almost forgot," he gasped. "You don't know the password and I don't want you to get killed coming out with the food."

That seemed sensible although he didn't mention what, if any, danger I might incur on the return trip. "What's the password?" I asked.

"Drop dead," he explained, without awareness of irony, and was off to the war.

Only a game can offer opportunities like that with a comforting insurance against untoward consequences. He enjoyed it, I enjoyed it and presumably the army enjoyed it. They ate the sandwiches, and nobody, including the cook, was scathed.

The indispensable ingredient of any game worth its salt is that the children themselves play it and, if not its sole authors, share in its creation. Watching TV's ersatz battles is not the same thing at all. Children act out their emotions, they don't talk them out and they don't watch them out. Their imagination and their muscles need each other. What imagination incites, action releases. No one can dream a child's dreams for him. No one can create the dramas that answer the needs of his own soul. No one can play for him the games that spend the body's energy in the service of his own growth and transformation from the primitive to all that we call civilized. That is the tragedy of the endless TV stare, that it substitutes the synthetic for the genuine, the mass production for the creative and individual. A game can transform the action that is destructive into the drama that spends itself without damage to themselves and others, but it must be the child's own game, created, directed and played by him.

Despite the bitter lessons of human history, adults do not yet appreciate the wonderful power of this translation. The small boy plays Superman and spreads his makebelieve wings in the happy illusion of power. He plays a dozen stories with zest and relish, occasionally to the considerable annoyance of his elders. The Nazis played Superman too, but they were grownups, at least biologically, and the illusion had warped into humorless delusion. The consequences all the world knows.

Of all the games that children enjoy, none delight them so much as those they share with the grownup who possesses the precious gift of gaiety. Gaiety is surely one of the loveliest qualities in the human lexicon of emotion. It has no thread of cruelty, no tinge of destructiveness, no clumsiness of pretense.

Spontaneous, generous, light-footed it sparkles with life and is always and forever the enemy of the dark corners of the human soul. It has no part in the artificial, hectic hullabaloos that try so sadly to imitate its inimitable spirit. It flowers in the small events of every day, without champagne and music for accompaniment. It has its own gallantry, and it flies its own flags.

There was the small boy who was sternly told to wash his hands before dinner. That particular day he was not in the mood to comply. He had no basic objection to hand-washing, at least within reasonable limits, but like everyone else he had his moments when he preferred to say "No" simply because he felt like "No." His mother settled down for a struggle, and the situation threatened to deteriorate into one of those tugs-of-war that plague both grownups and children over who is going to have the final word. At the crucial moment a friend remarked to the angry small belligerent, "Did you ever notice what water says when you turn the faucet and let it come out?"

The little boy looked at her suspiciously but admitted that this was an observation that had so far escaped him. Also, he liked the idea that he permitted or didn't permit something to happen, even if it was only water from a faucet. "Try it and listen," urged his friend. That much he agreed to although in no wise was this to be construed as a consent to hand-washing. He listened intently while his grown-up friend wove a cheerful echo to the water's happy rush for freedom. The whole game delighted him, and soap merely added a froth of foam to the carefree sound. His hands were immaculate, his mother was calling him to dinner and everyone was laughing. Only gaiety was wise enough to know that running water can tell charming thoughts to a small boy.

The people with that special gift you remember all your
life with the particular glow of happiness that once lit up a
child's world. I remember a neighbor that all of us on our
street visited regularly. As soon as school was out, we stopped
at her house on the way home. In winter she had hot cocoa
ready, and in warm weather there was always a pitcher of
lemonade. What we talked about was no more than the events
of the day, but by some magic those mundane activities became exciting, touched with adventure and mysterious possibilities. We all laughed because suddenly they seemed bursting
with comic twists and angles. Our grown-up friend enjoyed
them too, and she had stories of her own day, bright with
color and humor. None of the stories were unusual and I suppose there was nothing brilliant about our conversation. That
was not important, then or now. What was wonderful for all
of us was that everything looked different when we were
with her. You found yourself laughing about the argument
that had made you boiling mad an hour before. The grievance
you had been cherishing all day dwindled into oblivion and
what had been too dull for notice developed unexpected
points of interest.

I remember we almost never quarreled when we were
with her. It wasn't that we were making any great effort to be
angelic. We were feeling too happy and peaceful to be bothered with the usual incitements to battle. She seemed to have
any amount of time for us, and we had that wonderful feeling
that there was no need to hurry a story before adult attention
slid away to grown-up affairs. The party usually broke up
because a mother called to say it was time Mary and John
came home. Looking back from the distant vantage point of
adulthood I suppose she had her problems and faults like anyone else, but for us she was the fairy godmother who invited

us into an enchanted world that had always the clarity of reality. With her we liked ourselves and each other. Grownups sometimes seek that magic in a cocktail. We found it with a cup of cocoa and a glass of lemonade, and none of us will ever forget.

Perhaps our modern world is too busy, too harassed for gaiety. It takes time and relaxation to be gay and freedom to concentrate on the small delights. It is strange, too, that children almost never find that enchanted world without a fairy godmother or godfather to lead the way. There must be a Pied Piper to play the happy song that woos the hearts of the young. Their elders hear only the echo of an old nostalgia.

The young are still available to gaiety. They recognize it instantly, never mistake it for any of its synthetic imitations. Unlike their elders they never confuse it with noise or jokes or tricks. I remember a little girl who had spent a gay and happy afternoon with a grownup she loved. They had been working together on creating a new doll's house, sharing the problems and triumphs of creation. As they finished, she sighed peacefully, "This has been a happy house today." Then she remembered that only that morning she had had a fight with her brother and sister who had left to pursue their own affairs. "I think," she remarked cheerfully, "that I had better go and make some friends." It is a pity the grown-up world cannot go and do likewise.

From stepping on a caterpillar to a pie in the face to the needle precision of satire to the laughter that is the heart of sanity the procession is one of life's greatest and most wonderful dramas. Its potential is new with every child born and its denial in the world's indifference is one of the world's great tragedies. We know tears. We have yet to learn laughter.

There Is
a Time for Everything

OF ALL the wonderful things about the wonderful and crazy human race the most promising is the urge to grow. Every child is born with it although in some it is more insistent. There is physical growth and intellectual growth and emotional growth, and each is a part of the other. When they all move together, the result is harmony. When one outstrips the other, there is conflict.

As in all of life, growth requires an environment, a soil, a climate, a balance. For the human young that must be provided by adults with steadiness and continuity for a span of years. For every parent this means restrictions, responsibilities, conflicts of interest and most of all, continuing accessibility to the young. Few things are harder on the modern mother than the unremitting demands of small children. In the past when relatives lived close and families wove the generations into one fabric there were more people to share those demands and dilute their impact. Now one person may have to absorb most of them with as small respite as the afternoon nap. To meet them with patience, fulfill the near-insatiable needs, maintain perspective, relax with the present while facing the future is a monumental demand upon any adult. Yet children must seek the fulfillment of needs in response to the imperious requirements of growth.

They are curious and so their questions are endless, but curiosity is a prelude to discovery. They are limited in knowledge so dangers must be foreseen, but the protected may become the protectors. They can do little for themselves so there must be constant care, but the cared-for may in their turn nurture the weak. They are superbly self-centered so they are oblivious to the needs and wants of others, but out of self-concentration may grow the quiet devotion of giving. They have an energy like a small sun forever renewing itself, but energy is the dynamo of achievement. They absorb love and attention the way a sponge absorbs water, but love ingested must renew itself in loving.

Of all the demands our day makes upon parents none is more insistent than this requirement of love. We treat it as a kind of social obligation that leaps into life full-grown without flaw or struggle. We assume it is a simple emotion that like the air is always with us. We're sure we know what it is so we rarely question what we mean. We say this child got into trouble because he was loved too much and that child got into trouble because he was loved too little. Presumably the others didn't get into trouble because they were loved just the right amount.

Yet love is a quality much more than a quantity. In the small child it is need fulfilled just as hatred is need denied. It is warm milk in his stomach, the touch of familiar hands, the sound of a familiar voice in the dark. It is shared laughter and the sputter of a familiar joke and the knowledge of safety. It is the experience of gentleness and strength continued. The child's love, still new and primitive, is impulsive, vacillating, self-centered. It is like the little boy who hearing his mother complain of a headache was moved to comfort her. Impulsively and in faithful imitation of his own experience he stroked her forehead murmuring gently, "Poor Mommy, poor Mommy." Then abruptly he pushed her away and said crisply, "That's enough."

From that to the love of maturity is a long and difficult struggle of growth. It is the most civilized and the most complex of all emotions. Probably no adult ever totally outgrows elements of that early primitive love. The emotional grownup has with struggle and help transformed most of it into perceptive and enduring concern for the loved one. That love is not blind because it is based on reality not fantasy. It has no need to deny the flaws of the loved one because loyalty is woven into its fabric, and illusion can only weaken the ability to protect. It is not, as we sometimes think, indulgence. Indulgence corrupts, as every "spoiled child" is witness to, because it is a hostage to indifference, an expiation for denial. Love is concerned with fulfillment not possession.

Very few grownups achieve it in its finest state. Some people scarcely take the first step. The most of us struggle somewhere in between. It begins with need fulfilled, with being loved. It grows to self-respect and self-liking. Because love expands, as hate contracts, it widens the circle to include others. It is never static, and it is always an affirmation of life. It trusts the urge to growth as the essential life force and knows that the great task is to direct that force. Life repays

that trust. "As He loves the arrow that is swift so He loves
the bow that is stable."

I will never forget a woman I saw only once and talked
with no more than an hour. A mother and a grandmother, she
looked her age, and her face carried the marks of living. It
was the contentment in her face that drew my attention because contented faces are rare. We talked as strangers sometimes do about the things that really mattered to us. She told
me presently, "I've had a good life. It hasn't always been easy
or pleasant, but it's had a lot of happiness too. The hardest
thing I had to take was losing my son in the war. That
brought me great grief, but it's been a comfort to know that
until he went away his life was a happy one. Before he went, I
told him that no matter what happened, I wanted him to
know that I'd always be grateful to life for giving him to me.
He brought me so much joy and nothing could take that
away." That woman had the rarest of qualities, the wisdom of
the heart.

There is no such thing as perfect love in this world. There
is only the struggle to grow and to keep trying. In the final
analysis there are only two kinds of people, those who try and
those who don't. The adult who loves children as they would
be loved also likes them and himself. He respects them not
only for what they may become but for what they are, and he
has the courage to try to learn who and what they are. It is
one of life's interesting paradoxes that no one can really respect another simply for his future potential. There's no escaping the effort, time and energy that finally enable one to
understand a different perspective on life, even one that has
been left behind.

There, of course, lies the root of the trouble. So much has
not been left behind and is out of season. "There is a time for

everything," sang the prophet. There is a time for childhood and a time for maturity, and the tragedy lies in their confusion. What is right and natural for the two-year-old either grows or corrupts with the years. What is out of season can only clash. It has lost its fit, its harmony with what is. For children the climate of growth is the harmony of maturity in season.

For grownups that is the meaning of happiness. Their troubles with children arise from the children they were and still are, from the perspectives that are out of season for the child's world and have never grown to fit the demands of the grown-up world. That makes for ever greater difficulty because the demands of our day become ever more complex. Human nature is contagious, and the adult world passes on the virus of its defects as it does the seed of its virtues. The more complex and insistent the demands of that world the greater the failures are and the more devastating their consequences for children and grownups alike. There is little use in screaming that parents are not what they once were. Neither is the world what it once was, and that is a good thing. Grownups have not, for at least a very long time, found it easy to understand the world in which they lived as children and which they unwittingly carried in bits and pieces into the alien land of adulthood. Nor do adults now, any more than before, live in a climate which encourages that understanding and respects the realities of that early world.

When we consider children important in their own right and valuable for their own sake, the climate of understanding will have a chance to grow. We will not need sentimentality because we will not fear disillusionment. With reality we can grow. When we grow, the children will grow also.